You Can't
Apologize
to a Dawg!

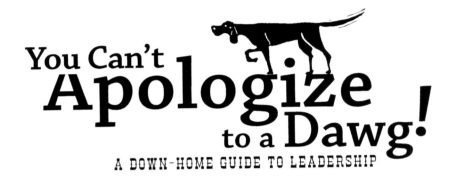

You Can't Apologize to a Dawg!

A DOWN-HOME GUIDE TO LEADERSHIP

TUCKER CHILDERS

PMP

Performance Management Publications (PMP)

Performance Management Publications (PMP)
3353 Peachtree Road NE, Suite 920
Atlanta, Georgia 30326
678.904.6149

International Standard Book Number: 0-937-100-13-7

Printed in the United States of America

2 3 4 5 6 7

Cover and text design by Lisa Smith

PMP is a division of Aubrey Daniels International, Inc.
PMP books are available at special discounts for bulk pur-
chases by corporations, institutions, and other organizations.
For more information, please call 678.904.6140, ext. 131, or
e-mail lglass@aubreydaniels.com.

To Camp,
A better son than I had hoped for
and the best friend I ever had.

Acknowledgments

To

Dr. Aubrey C. Daniels for providing me entrance into
"The Life" of Applied Behavior Analysis;

Courtney Mills whose obsession with
the science rubbed off on me;

Philip Hurst who encouraged me to start this book;

Gail Snyder, my editor, for encouraging me to finish it;

and those with whom I have worked over the years—
Sweet Betty, my good friend Byron,
the very special B.J., and all the rest:

Thank you so much.

Foreword

For over 30 years Tucker Childers has called me from time to time and announced, "I've got one for you." He will then proceed to tell me a joke or something funny that he saw, heard, read, or thought. He can't tell you anything without laughing. He is one who sees humor in everything.

He called me one day and I asked, "What do you have on your mind, Tucker?" "I just wanted to call and see if behavior is still a function of its consequences," he replied. When I told him that it was, he replied, "That makes me feel better. I'll talk to you later."

Because he looks for the funny side of everything, he clearly sees things that others don't, and that is in large part what made him an excellent coach for supervisors, managers, and executives with business issues. Years ago he was a consultant in a Milliken textile plant with serious problems. Costs were high, production was erratic, and personnel turnover was in excess of 200% annually. By introducing behavior management methods, he helped the plant meet its five-year goals in less than six months. Tucker worked primarily with frontline supervisors in this plant, but the positive changes in performance caused upper managers to use the behavioral jargon even though in many instances they used it inaccurately and inappropriately. One day Tucker was in the office of Mr. Alfred New, a division President and as they were talking, one of his plant mangers called. Mr. New, who was very old, started ranting and raving about something. In the middle of his fit, he looked at Tucker and paused mid-sentence. In his slow Southern drawl, he said to his plant manager Harry Balding, "Harry, our behavioral scientists tell us that we need to give four positives to every negative." He paused. "Now I've just chewed you out on two counts. Let me think. Oh well, I can't think of anything, I owe you eight."

Tucker and I worked together at ADI for close to a quarter century. No matter how many of my presentations he sat through, he would always come up at the break or end of the session with a story on one or more points that I made. On one particular day I talked about the fact that one positive reinforcer doesn't make a habit, that it takes many more than most people think. At the break, he related a story about Coach Wally Butts, his football coach at the University of Georgia. Coach Butts was the stereotype of a hard-nosed, old-school kind of coach. He was a beer drinking, cigar smoking, foul mouthed, out of shape, yelling, screaming kind of guy. Tucker related the following. "One day in practice, one of the backs ran a play and Coach Butts jumped all over him with both feet. When his ranting subsided, the player protested, "Coach Butts if there is one play I know, it was that one and I know I am supposed to block that man." The player said this with such conviction Coach Butts paused, looked at the backfield coach and asked, "That right?" The backfield coach replied, "Yes, Coach Butts he's right." Coach Butts looked at the player for a moment and said nothing. As he walked away, he muttered, "Humph, knows one damn play and wants me to make him a Phi Beta Kappa."

In this book, Tucker relates many of his experiences from growing up in Dalton, GA to consulting with many of the top corporations in America. All are humorous and all have a lesson in leadership. Learning and having fun. What a novel idea.

— **Aubrey C. Daniels, Ph.D.**
Aubrey Daniels International

Introduction

When I graduated from college in 1963, I hadn't taken any courses on how to lead people. Back then, such courses weren't even offered. Once I entered the world of work, it didn't take long to discover that this was a serious omission in my preparation for life, so I set out to fill-in that particular blank by talking with people who seemed good at leadership. It was amazing how little useable information I got. One old-timer offered, "Young man, leading and managing others isn't a thing in the world but keeping all the balls in the air." That may sound weak, but it changed my life. My young bride was aware of my frustration and we discussed it often. One day as a joke, she bought me a copy of a book called *Juggling for the Complete Klutz* and included a card that said "LOOK OUT WORLD!" Guess what? I learned to juggle. However, the result was fairly discouraging since this new skill did not improve my leadership abilities and, to make matters worse, nobody wanted to watch me juggle. You might expect that children, at least, would enjoy watching someone juggle. They couldn't care less. I discontinued my efforts after the first half of the book, which was after the three-ball juggle and before the four-ball juggle. Get ready. Here comes the first.

LEADER'S LAW: You can learn to do just about anything if you are willing to pay the price, but make sure the end result is worth the price you have to pay. If no one wanted to see me juggle three balls, why would they want to see me juggle four? People in business call that "return on investment." Will the return justify the expense?

The other thing I learned is that learning does not have to be hard work. The effort can be less than you would imagine. Leadership can be defined in many ways, but the definition I prefer is "getting things done through others." And the reality is "it just ain't that tough."

— Tucker Childers

Disclaimer #1: I use the pronouns he, his, and him predominantly throughout the book. This isn't because I think women aren't excellent leaders or potential leaders. I know they are. They're also good sports and will hopefully understand that it's just too confusing for me to keep switching back and forth.

Disclaimer #2: Believe it or not, the first names in this book were **not** changed to protect the innocent people who were saddled with them at birth.

Table of Contents

ONE

If It Looks Like a Duck and Quacks Like a Duck, It May Be a Duck

*Nothing great was ever achieved
without enthusiasm.*

Ralph Waldo Emerson, Circles in Essays: First Series 1841

Inspire. Energize. Lead. These words go hand in hand. We look up to people who make us want to achieve accomplishments. They motivate us in ways that others simply can't. Creating *motivation* is at the heart of any good leader. Unfortunately, the word motivation has been altered over the years. To most people it brings about grand visions like the father of six who, after attending a rally and listening to some motivational tapes, quit his job and sold three million dollars worth of vitamin supplements in only three weeks. He now has a sales force of sixty and spends his days on the beach in Costa del Sol working on his tan.

Motivation is an important word as is the word *motive* from whence it came, but both seem to have accumulated a bit of baggage over the years. To discover someone's motivation seems to imply that we have to get inside his/her mind which is a place where we usually are not welcome and I have no desire to go anyway. The word *reason* makes more sense. People have *reasons* for what they do. Essentially the reason people do what they do is because their actions bring some sort of positive consequence for them. These consequences can usually be observed which is much easier and more accurate than trying to discover a person's internal motivation. This concept is also seen in the animal world. For example, a dog begs if it eventually gets a treat for doing so. We don't have to know what the dog is thinking if we simply examine the consequences of the dog's actions.

Anything a person does, he does because he has a reason. It may not be a good reason in our opinion, but it was good enough for him at the time. John Wesley Hardin, a gunfighter in the Old West, once shot a man for snoring. That may strike you as being a bit on the harsh side, but who are we to judge? What we need to realize is that when we see twelve people engaged in the same activity, they could each have different reasons for participating. This is important to remember because *leadership is getting things done through others.* The task then becomes providing reasons for people to expend their efforts in a way that will help you to achieve your goals. It isn't as difficult as it sounds. And, it sure as heck is much easier than performing a questionable analysis of somebody's internal motivation.

This slight change of worldview from motivation to reason creates a foundation that profoundly changes how you deal with people. These small conceptual differences really hit home for me when I was sitting around one night with a few of my friends playing music. Jack Weeks was, in my opinion, the best fiddler who ever drew a bow across a string. Somebody asked him, "So, Jack, what's the difference between a violin and a fiddle?" His answer was quite profound. "A violin has *strings* and a fiddle has *strangs.*" Jack's fine discrimination changed his approach to how he played the instrument. Similarly, in order to motivate others, you need to know where and how to inspire individuals to say, "Now you're playing my song!"

 **LEADER'S LAW: To be a leader and get people excited, create good reasons for people to follow you.**

Now that we know what we need to do–provide reasons to create motivation–let's begin to look at some ways to do it. What are some qualities of leadership that we can identify and build into our own behavior? Let's be honest here. It matters how you look. If you look like a leader, you have a leg up on the rest of us.

Close your eyes for a minute (but wait until you finish reading this paragraph) and visualize a leader. What does he look like? What is he doing? How are people responding to him? Okay, now close your eyes for a minute.

My vision is one that we have all seen hundreds of times. It's that wonderful painting of Washington crossing the Delaware. Dead winter. Ice floating in the water. George standing in front of the boat facing the shore. He looked great. He was a tall guy, about six foot five I read someplace. In that painting, he has a look of absolute determination on his face and his dress is impeccable. All of this was topped off by the perfect hat. The hat *made* him. This is an exemplary picture of leadership.

Since there were no videos or cameras in those days, we have to assume that the artist painted his own vision of the event and I think he did a terrific job. He knew how a leader was supposed to look. He somehow brought out the qualities of courage and strength. You notice that George was not wearing a propeller beanie or a baseball cap. That wouldn't have worked at all. Also, his snappy suit and his determined expression would not have worked nearly as well if he had been sitting down in the back of the boat. I have a feeling that if he had been wearing the propeller beanie and sitting in the back of the boat, today we might all be eating shepherd's pie and sending birthday cards to the Queen.

Some of our physical characteristics, of course, are things that we simply can't do anything about. It helps to be tall and I have tried everything I know to do to gain a little bit in that area. Alas, five foot nine is the best I can do. I can do other things, however, to improve my edge. You may think that I'm talking through my hat here, but I can prove it.

A colleague of mine, while in graduate school at Georgia State University, was required to do a project on this very subject. The process was very creative and the result, I think you will agree, is a real eye-opener. After finding three friends who were willing to help, he was off and running. Friend #1 wore a tie-dyed T-shirt, torn jeans, and no shoes; he hadn't shaved for a week and was in serious need of a haircut. His job was to stand on a busy street corner in downtown Atlanta and cross the street *against* the light. My colleague's job was to count the number of people who walked across the street with Friend #1. This was an easy job because not one person did so. Several people made uncomplimentary comments, but since he was not counting remarks, that hard data is lost forever.

Friend #2 dressed a bit better: khaki pants, golf shirt, Wejuns– in other words, frat boy attire. Guess what? When he crossed the street against the light, a few people followed him out into the traffic. He crossed several times and the results were similar.

Friend #3 dressed as the dandy. He wore a three-piece suit with a conservative red tie and a pair of wingtips. His briefcase matched his shoes. When he crossed the street against the light, how many people do you think followed him? ALL OF THEM! What does this mean? More than likely, it means that people look for something in others that conveys confidence and knowledge. In the *absence* of knowing you, people will look for any available cues, especially those they can get from your appearance.

 **LEADER'S LAW: Realize that folks look for leaders in every situation.**

Everyone has his or her own taste in clothes. Everyone makes a statement with the clothes they wear. For most people, one's fashion lets others know what kind of people you like to be with. Of course, this isn't true for all people. There is an exception to every rule. I once knew a man who liked the look of new clothes so much that he wore them only once and then disposed of them. I don't know what he did with his discarded clothes, but if he were my size I would certainly have looked into it.

My son, on the other hand, used to frequently shop at Goodwill Industries. Not only were the clothes reasonably priced, but he didn't have to endure the discomfort of new clothes during their "seasoning" process which can take upwards to five or six years. Both are examples of people who made a statement about their values by how they dressed.

My son was proud that he could get a pair of $25 jeans for around 25¢ and he could wear them for at least a year or so, maybe two years if he could get his hands on some duct tape. His fashion choice, I think, had a great deal to do with his choice of careers. His style has elevated a couple of notches to be more consistent with those around him, but for the most part it remains casual. Today, he is an associate director for several television programs. Actually, he looks a lot like the people with whom he works. Several people report to him on a daily basis and since he gets things done through others, he fits our definition of a leader even though he doesn't have a hat like George Washington's.

The military has always been notable for its development of effective leaders. Did you ever notice that most soldiers dress the same? During Desert Storm, I always looked forward to General Swartzkoph's nightly briefings. There's a leader for you. He was cool, calm, and dressed smartly in his desert camouflage. If he had been wearing a Japanese kimono and a baseball cap, my dedication to catching his act might not have been as great. But his fashion matched the seriousness of his message. One look at him and you immediately knew the topic.

In terms of fashion, small things make a difference. Small things convey important messages about who you are and what you believe and value.

 **LEADER'S LAW: Everybody's image speaks to who they are, or are not.**

When you're a leader, people look to see if what you *say,* what you *do,* and what you *wear* match.

Did you ever hear of a man named Yother Bean? Probably not. I have to tell you up front that Yother was a bit exceptional. For example, he told everyone that during World War II, he was a quiet leader and served as General Eisenhower's chief intelligence officer. He claimed to actually have in his possession, though I never personally saw it, Hitler's best china along with tea service and Tojo's actual table settings made of pure platinum. He managed to get these prizes because he was the first American to enter Japan and he went straight to Tojo's house. Then he went to Germany and proceeded directly to Hitler's place. Being a high-ranking military man, he took what he wanted. How do I know? He told me. Yother wouldn't lie. However, I do know for a fact that Yother has never set foot outside of North Georgia.

I'll never forget the day that Yother broke the news to me about his extensive real estate holdings. He actually believed that he owned every house in North Georgia. Every one of them! One day Yother was walking by our place and he didn't look pleased at all. My mom yelled, "Hey, Yother. It's a hot day. Why don't you sit down there under the tree and I'll bring you a glass of lemonade."

Yother replied, "I don't have time today. I'm in a business crisis."

I decided to walk along with him for a ways and see if I could find out what the problem was. He didn't keep me waiting long. He said, "You know that I own every house in North Georgia?" I nodded and he went on to say, "Well, I found out last week there's one I don't own."

You could have knocked me over with a feather. "No kiddin'! Which one?"

He said, "West Morris Street at Thornton Avenue and don't ask me how that happened 'cause I don't know and I'm on my way to find out right now."

This did not seem like a really big problem to me. I suggested, "Shoot, Yother. Why don't you just stop by there and buy it?"

He said, "I made them an offer the other day and they say it ain't for sale. I declare, if this business keeps up it'll be a pure miracle if I don't come down with a ulcerated stomach."

Yother never made it to the heights of leadership that he probably deserved. I think the problem may have been the bib overalls and the John Deere tractor cap, coupled with the fact that what he said to people didn't match with observable reality.

LEADER'S LAW: You can say important things, but in and of itself that alone doesn't mean too much. If you talk a good game, but have no evidence to back it up, you won't be a leader for long . . . if ever.

What you *do* is who you are. No leader can hide from his or her actions. Sooner or later you will be associated with the message (good or bad) that you bring, or become known as the person who only talks a good game. A good leader makes it his mission to live his message.

Budgie Bean, Yother's brother, was a classmate of mine in the fifth grade, and his claim to fame was that he beat up every boy in the school. Since he was seventeen, the easy part was beating up all of the boys. The hard part was making sure he didn't miss anybody. The fact that he pulled it off was a testament to his organizational skills and goal orientation. As evidence of his rearing as a Southern gentleman, he didn't beat up but a few of the girls.

Like Yother, he had a head for commerce. He went into the business of selling deferments. He'd say, "Okay, Fat Boy, you can take your whoopin' right now or you can give me a quarter and take your whoopin' tomorrow." Conservative custodianship of funds has been one of my family's traditions since before I was born and it continues to this day. Therefore, I elected to take my whoopin' right then. That level of fiscal responsibility is not common in eleven-year-old boys and I was proud that I had made that choice. Besides, I didn't have a quarter and Budgie didn't understand or embrace the concept of credit terms and easy payment plans.

I don't know whatever happened to Budge. He didn't finish out the year. He had reached his goal of whipping all the boys by Thanksgiving and his interest in remaining on the school grounds began to wane. When the principal told him that after Christmas break he would no longer be permitted to park his truck in the teachers' parking lot, (such facilities were not generally provided for fifth graders) he never came back. I thought all the Beans had potential, because they seemed to believe their own stories and carried through with promised threats. However, they appeared to lack judgment in selecting images and missions that would prove successful for the long term. At least, Budgie was a man of his word.

LEADER'S LAW: If you manage behavior with power and threats, people will do what you demand . . . until they figure out how to escape, avoid you, or cause your downfall.

In addition to examining your image, deciding if what you say aligns with what you do, and determining if you have a good mission, people will look to see how you make decisions. Are decisions based on what you believe is just common sense or do you make decisions based on a more rational method?

Is there anybody more irritating than a person who knows everything? I'm thinking of Cliff from the old *Cheers* TV series. The only difference in Cliff and real-life know-it-alls is Cliff was funny. Most know-it-alls are not. I heard it said once that all people serve their fellow man if only by providing a bad example.

Ambrose is one person who, when I look back, had a profound impact on me. Every time I have a birthday, I sit down and try to take a realistic look at myself and my behavior. Then I say a short prayer. "Oh Lord, please keep an eye on me this year. Don't let me slip into the Ambrose groove."

Ambrose looked like a person who had done something right. He looked like a leader. He was tall, well dressed, with hair graying at the temples, and he displayed an air of aristocracy. The parts that showed were impressive. The parts that didn't show caused all the trouble.

When I met him, he was a VP of a fairly large company and by legislation then, a designated leader. He had worked for this company all his life and as he was getting into his sixties, he spent less and less time contributing and more and more time looking for loopholes in the company retirement policy. People were beginning to avoid him. He had changed his role to "learned councilor" and enjoyed the new position he had created for himself. The problem was that his council was seldom what the counselee wanted to hear, so his advice was consequently ignored. I asked him one day what he planned to spend his time doing once he retired. He smiled and settled back to dispense some Ambrose wisdom.

"I'm going to write a book. It should sell millions of copies, because everyone needs it and it will be beneficial to all those who use it. The name of the book will be Don't Try It. I Already Did and It Didn't Work. In all of my years in this business, I've had every possible idea. I've followed through on all of them and almost all of them failed. Whenever the reader has an idea, all they have to do is look it up and the information will be right there to tell them why their idea won't work. The book will probably need to be two or three volumes. It can't miss. It will be my legacy."

When Ambrose finally retired, his co-workers threw a big party and gave him a good send-off. There was a question in my mind, however, as to exactly what they were really celebrating. I recall that Bear Bryant, the legendary coach of the University of Alabama, sent a graduation present to Tucker Fredrickson, the great running back from Auburn University who had run roughshod over his defense for the past three years. He enclosed a tongue-in-cheek card that said, "Let there be no mistake. I am sincerely happy to see you graduate—even happier than your Mama and Daddy."

Just because somebody tried something and it didn't work doesn't mean that you can discount it. All of Ambrose's ideas cannot be discounted as failures simply because he threw something out and it didn't work the way he presented it. The key is to create a method that can show what you change and how you changed it *(one step at a time)* until success is achieved. That's what I call making decisions rationally.

Ambrose never wrote the book.

 **LEADER'S LAW: Common sense ain't so common. Truly good leaders have a method for showing people how to make good ideas happen.**

TWO

Born Leaders . . . Can We Isolate That Gene?

Be not afraid of greatness.
Some are born great,
some achieve greatness,
and some have greatness thrust upon them.

Shakespeare, Twelfth Night, II, v

Throughout the centuries great thinkers have argued back and forth about the root "causes" of leadership. Simply put, some believe that people are born to be leaders, while others believe that we have to learn the skills to be a leader. Regardless of whether you think this difference is important or not, our everyday conversations tend to be full of sayings that reflect the influence of these differing points of view. For example, following are a few comments that many of us have heard all our lives:

"I tell ya, the man is a born leader."

"Look for great things from that boy; he's a born winner."

"He's got that sinking curve ball just like his daddy had. They won't hit much off him."

"The apple doesn't fall far from the tree."

"Her mother had the heart of a lion and I can see that she inherited one just like it."

"Their daddy was the laziest man I ever saw. You can't expect much more from those kids."

These are just a few examples that support the idea that great leaders come from great leaders. If that is true, then loser parents can produce nothing better than loser children. People sometimes accept this as true because it happens so often. You're probably thinking of exceptions right now, and I am happy to say that exceptions are not uncommon. Yes, there will always be a preacher's kid doing three-to-five for sticking up a 7-Eleven store, or a drug-addicted daughter of a policeman. But, one can also find the person who beat the odds by becoming a captain of industry while his or her parents never did anything more productive than make moonshine.

From my point of view, the behavior that I think is important for leaders is not genetic. Leadership skills are learned.

I am not a geneticist and have never claimed to be one. I don't need to be one because there are already many fine ones out there who go to work every day and earn a comfortable living by researching and learning more and more things about what genes really do. But they haven't yet found the genes that make a person better at earning money, playing cards, leading large numbers of people, hunting, fishing, or stealing chickens. People *learn* to do these things.

 **LEADER'S LAW: If you watch the right people, you can catch on to this leadership stuff.**

Getting good things to happen to people when they are doing what you ask from them is not without its puzzles or backfires. Sometimes people place too much reliance upon their recollection of behaviors that have been rewarded in the past. A good example of this is the time our deputy sheriff arrested an elephant.

In our county, anyone caught speeding received a citation and was expected to pay the fine immediately. Sometimes the offender could not pay and, in those cases, the vehicle was impounded until the offender paid. This rule did not apply to locals, of course, since they would come by sooner or later to settle up. It was aimed primarily at the out-of-towner who was just passing through, especially any vehicle that displayed a New York license plate.

One night our deputy stopped a truck that was passing through and the driver said, "I ain't got no money." The deputy employed the same procedure that he had used many times in the past. The problem was that either he failed to notice or neglected to recognize that impounding a truck is dramatically different from impounding a truck that has an elephant in the back.

You can't just park an elephant and wait for the owner to come by to pay his fine and pick him up. The impoundment lot adjoined the county jail and the prisoners began to complain about the smell almost immediately. Elephants are notoriously indifferent in regard to their selection of an appropriate place to let nature take its course. And in this case, at least, the elephant had no choice. The jailer was assigned the job of shoveling out the lot every hour or so.

Of course, elephants are well known to be hearty eaters. This elephant required at least three or four bales of hay every day or he would get upset and make threatening moves toward the chain-link fence. Worst of all, he drew a crowd. Very few people in the county had ever seen a live elephant up close and most were determined to get a good look at him before he made bail and got released. Teachers brought their classes and I expect that everyone in North Georgia came at least once to see this interesting creature. The sheriff, known as R. C., was very sensitive to the political implications of this whole affair because of comments such as, "What kind of a sheriff impounds elephants?" His stress level was at an all-time high and all because his deputy had followed orders and did what he had always done—issue citations to speeders.

Sheriff R. C. was an organized, by-the-book lawman, and he didn't like these little bumps that had the potential to grow bigger. He was faced with a dilemma here that would test the limits of his creativity. He ran the department on a strict budget and there was no place for hay or the delivery of same. R. C. had officially impounded the elephant as a vehicle (since he had seen a picture of somebody riding an elephant, so it met the criteria) but there was no budget category for feeding vehicles. There appeared to be only one solution. The sheriff arrested the elephant, charging it with being an accessory to a traffic violation. Now he could charge the hay to the "food for prisoners" budget.

The next problem was staying within the food for prisoners budget. Even the most conservative Republican would admit that the food allowance in our county jail was a bit meager. R. C. solved this problem by giving early release to Coot Green and Waco Paul who each had ten days remaining on drunk and disorderly convictions. Both of them were livid at the prospect of being displaced with practically no notice. More than anything, I think, they both had their feelings hurt. Coot was the spokesman for the two when he said, "Startin' today, me and Waco are gonna throw all our business to Murray County. Sheriff Poag knows how to treat his good customers." This problem would have to be addressed at a later date.

A week had passed when the elephant's owner walked into the sheriff's office. Had it been Santa Claus who walked in, the sheriff could not have been happier to see him. His smile vanished quickly, though, when the man announced, "I still ain't got no money and the truck ain't got no gas."

The sheriff was a man known for his flexibility and fast thinking. He dropped the charges against the driver, sentenced the elephant to time served, filled the truck's tank at the county pump and threw in four bales of hay for the road. Then he wrote a memo for immediate posting on the bulletin board at the office. It said, "This ain't no damn zoo. Don't EVER impound another animal. If you do, you will be very sorry." To my knowledge, nobody ever did do it again, especially with elephants.

The point is that people (and animals, for that matter) do things because they have a reason. If we want a person to do something, all we have to do is give him a reason to do it. Make him or her glad they did it and then they have a reason for doing it again. The deputy in this case had received a lot of praise for giving out-of-towners traffic tickets and impounding their goods as collateral. The sheriff had probably slapped him on the back many times for bringing in extra cash to the county, so eventually the deputy gave tickets and impounded possessions no matter what the circumstances.

 **LEADER'S LAW: Be careful of and specific about what you encourage and reward folks to do, because they will do it again, sometimes in circumstances that you might not appreciate.**

Now for another word of caution: From simple beginnings, obsessive behavior grows.

Do you like dogs? I do. I'm never too busy to stop and talk to a dog. Dogs were an important part of the culture where I grew up and many of life's puzzles became clear from watching their response to everyday events. They have been, to me, a learning experience. They're honest, they have no hidden agenda, and they are normally right up front about their feelings in regard to things that are going on around them. They either like you or they don't and you don't usually have to guess which. Most of all, they do things for a reason, and the reason is normally obvious if we take the trouble to look. I say "normally" because I have never been able to identify the reason most dogs turn around three times before lying down. Maybe I'll try it myself, but I'm straying from my subject. What we are addressing here is how people and animals learn behavior. Let me describe an event that should give you a good example of how this happens.

When I was a youngster, my all-time favorite yard dog was named Junior. No one knew for sure who his father was so my assumption is that the choice of name was intended to make him feel good about himself. He was a happy dog and although he did not enjoy the level of respect that was reserved for hunting dogs, he took daily advantage of all social opportunities that arose. Those opportunities usually consisted of following the kids around and participating in their adventures. It was on one of these treks that Junior's life changed forever.

We kids were a mixed group in terms of gender, age, shape, and size, but Junior didn't care. He was along for whatever happened. One day, as we walked along a country path, a corn snake that had apparently been thinking about something else, slithered out in front of the group, and the girls started screaming. Now, corn snakes are harmless. They do, however, bear the same general appearance as a rattlesnake, and if that's not enough reason to scream I don't know what is. It was then that the amazing happened. Junior flew into action. He pounced on the snake. He not only pounced; he did grievous damage and began to systematically destroy that sucker while the girls kept up their screaming. When he got tired of dismantling the snake, he walked off the path and sat down.

The girls stopped screaming and started fawning over Junior. They stroked, hugged, and lavished praise on this animal that had never experienced this kind of attention in his entire life. When they finished, guess what Junior did? He went back to this pile of greasy tissue that used to be a snake and proceeded to inflict further damage. When he finished his second assault, the girls repeated their treatment. The rest is history. We now owned the only snake-dog in the state of Georgia (to my knowledge) and Junior's life had taken on a purpose that would continue until the day he died.

The reason he killed so many snakes, of course, was the treatment he received afterward. He loved the attention, but he could get it only when someone was present, not just Junior and the snake. The solution to this problem was one that I thought was creative. He would find a snake, kill it, and then bring the carcass of the dearly departed home and lay it in the yard. Then he would retire to a shady spot to wait for somebody to come by. When they did, he would get up and sit next to the former snake until someone noticed. There were two potential problems associated with his obsession: 1) if my mother had known where all those snakes were coming from, there was a good chance that Junior could have lost his job as family yard dog and been replaced by one with more acceptable behaviors, and 2) Junior's accidental learning experience did not include any information on discrimination skills. Rattlesnakes were very common in our area, but Junior only saw a snake, and that was all the information he needed. To Junior, a snake was just another variety of toy.

We all tried to reason with Junior, but it never did any good. My dad would say, "Junior, you're an idiot. One of these days you're going to attack a rattlesnake and it'll kill you." Then he would smile, bend over, and rub Junior on the head. It was sound advice that Junior refused to process. What he did process was the action of being rubbed on the head. He loved it and he would go back looking for snakes as soon as everyone left the yard. He never learned to discriminate and as a result was bitten several times by poisonous snakes. Some of these episodes must have caused a great deal of discomfort, but he kept on until the day he died many years later of natural causes.

The point of all this is that we are what we have learned to be because of the consequences we experience. If we are lucky, we find ourselves with people who recognize and reward us for doing good, productive things. If we learn that lesson then we may go on to inspire others to be productive as well.

 **LEADER'S LAW: Don't ever underestimate how powerful a little bit of attention can be. And don't ever underestimate what a person (or pet) is willing to do to get it.**

THREE

Good Banjo Players Spend a Lot of Time Tuning Their Banjos

Patience is the companion of wisdom.

St. Augustine, d. A.D. 430, On Patience

I've stated that, in my opinion, leaders are made, not born. There's no magic to it and the transition is not one that is accomplished through the skilled use of smoke and mirrors. If you undertake to become a leader, you may never get to say, "Today, I am one." What you should expect is a never-ending process of getting better and better, and I will say to you honestly, there may come a time when you will ask yourself, what's wrong with being a good follower? The answer to that question is "not a darn thing." To some extent, you get to decide which you want to be, but if a leader is something that you currently are not and you want to learn how, there's absolutely no reason to delay. Let's get to it. Time's a-wastin'.

First, let's do a brief skills assessment. Can you teach a chicken how to dance? If you can, you have a very good start. If you can't, don't be alarmed or discouraged. You may have not had that particular opportunity. However, we can grow this skill without a great deal of effort and strain on your part IF you're smarter than the chicken that has an I.Q. of about two points higher than a ball-peen hammer. I know that we have no problems in that regard. After all, you are reading this book which is a testament to your elevated intelligence.

Did you ever notice that there are some people who, when they walk into a room, everybody looks up and smiles? You may not have noticed this because you were smiling, too. Why is that? They haven't done or said anything, so why would we automatically smile? We smile for the same reason we smile when someone comes into the room on Thanksgiving Day carrying a golden brown turkey or into the break room carrying a dozen donuts. That little computer that we carry around in our heads says, "Wake up; something good is about to come your way."

The person who just entered has something we want and he has a history of dispensing it generously. It doesn't have to be a turkey or a box of donuts. It can be a simple comment or any demonstration of approval. This is plenty for most people. Perfection is rare, of course, and that is why a good banjo player is always tuning his banjo: it's never quite perfectly tuned. Everybody may smile and look forward to the carving of a turkey except for the person in the room who is chairman of C P S F P F T. (That's the "Coalition of People Supporting Fair Play for Turkeys.") And, a health enthusiast might prefer setting himself on fire to eating a donut. Of course, absolute perfection is very difficult to achieve in any endeavor, but getting better at it is almost always possible. Even an excellent leader can't please everybody; yet, the more pleasure you show in response to people's valued actions, the more people want to do the things that please you.

 **LEADER'S LAW:** The difference between folks wanting to see you or wanting you to go away depends on your skill at delivering good things–not suck-up things–sincere things.

Question: Are you a positive person who lets people know when they have done something that pleases you? In other words, have you given them a reason to do it again? Yes? That's what they all say, but that does not necessarily make it true. Not that people lie. Some people really do give others a reason to do something worthwhile while others just think they do. When we take the time to find out, we often find that we think good thoughts about people, but often stop short of telling them. Important point: You can think good thoughts about a person all day long, but unless he's The Great Kreskin, he'll never know that you're pleased without some outward demonstration of your approval. In other words, you gotta say so!

OK, time to get to work. Get yourself a three-by-five index card. Draw a line down the middle. (It doesn't need to be perfectly straight. We will not grade for neatness.) On the top left of the card, write the letter "A." On the top right, write the letter "D." The hard work is done. You may put it in your shirt pocket. Now, every time you make a statement of approval to anyone, take the card out and make a tick mark in the section under "A." It doesn't matter where you are or to whom you are speaking. Make the mark. Every time you make a statement of disapproval, take it out and put a tick mark in the section under "D." Again, it doesn't matter where you are or to whom you are speaking (spouse, child, employee, co-worker, boss, store clerk, family dog). Be honest! After a week of doing this, you will have collected enough data to begin work on a life-changing project.

The first thing you may notice is "Hey, there aren't any marks on this card!" Do not despair. This simply means that you don't make your feelings known as much as you probably should. (Either that or you completely forgot about the exercise.) This too is valuable and usable information. Here's an important point: when you don't demonstrate approval OR disapproval, *people assume disapproval.* If that doesn't put the pressure on you, I don't know what will. Now, unless you are one of those people who didn't make any marks, then get a clean card and start over. If you didn't make any tick marks, try to increase the tick marks this time.

On the other hand, if you have a large number of ticks on both sides of your card this indicates that you make a lot of comments and that is a good start. Add up all tick marks under "A" and all tick marks under "D." Then divide "A" by "D" and the answer is your *comment ratio.* If the answer is four or more approving remarks for every disapproving remark, you are probably one who generates a lot of smiles when you come into the room. If the answer is less than four approving comments to every one disapproving comment, then you need to tune the old banjo a bit (maybe a lot). If the answer is less than one positive comment, you now know why you weren't invited to join the bowling team or asked out to lunch lately.

Just remember that perfection is not a realistic goal. Even sincere statements of approval may not always be received the way we intend. "You play racquetball well for an older guy" has been one comment that never went over real well with me. Also avoid saying "You don't sweat much for a fat girl" unless you have really good reflexes and can dodge a quick right hook.

 **LEADER'S LAW: If you mean it, don't be so stingy with your recognition. And if you want to give people a reason to be more motivated, you have to be more positive than negative.**

Let's get back to the index card. Since I can't do anything for or to you if you do or don't use it, let me share a real-life experience. Back in the early 1970s, I was assigned consulting work at a textile plant that was owned by a large corporation. It was a very modern structure and looked great from the interstate. Inside, however, it was a different story. The plant was still modern and the machinery and equipment was state of the art; the problem was the numbers. Actual production efficiency was in the 40th percentile of expectations and everything else lounged around in the same neighborhood. Managers stated that the problem was attendance and if they could only get people to come to work on a regular basis, they could get production numbers up very quickly.

You may already know this, but in the event that you don't, I have a news flash. Attendance is rarely the main problem in any organization. Poor attendance, like a nagging cough, is a symptom of a problem. Barring a known epidemic of the Asian flu or some other current virus, people tend to stay out of work simply because they would rather be someplace else.

Work versus play. Which would we rather do? When work results in pay and play results in cost, the need to pay the bills tends to win the tug-of-war for our time. Yet, the more that we associate punishment with the job, the more attractive play becomes. Fortunately, the opposite is also true.

This was the early 1970s. This plant was producing textured yarn that was used to make double- knit fabric. This fabric was used to make stretch pants (normally plaid) and leisure suits (usually in some nauseating pastel color) which when complemented by white shoes and belt, then accessorized with some puka shell beads, made a real fashion statement. Believe it or not, the demand for this yarn (at the time) was so great that the company was actually making money.

The plant's managers had experienced some very basic problems that they managed to turn around in a very short time. In fact, their performance skyrocketed so high that the facility was written up on the front page of the local newspaper . . . except for one department. The boss of that department was a guy named John, and his employees hated him with a hope-he-breaks-his-back kind of hate. He had never spoken to me and he seemed a bit antisocial. The plant manager suggested that he meet with me and discuss some things that we might do to improve the performance in his department and perhaps even get people to come to work more often. I opened our conversation by diplomatically asking, "John, do you realize how much your employees hate you?" His reply was sad.

He said, "Yeah, I know it. I don't know what they want. I manage them just like I would like to be managed. If everything is OK, they never see me. If problems crop up, then I go huntin'. That means I find the person who's messing up and I make them wish they hadn't. Then I go away and they don't have to deal with me again until the next problem."

Is that a sad commentary? John really believed he was doing the right thing. In other words, no employee had to guess why he came to the production floor. The only question was who would be taken to the woodshed that day. When they saw John, they saw punishment coming at a full gallop.

 **LEADER'S LAW: When people don't want to work for you, there's probably a good reason why.**

The solution to John's problem was to create the possibility for his employees that he just might be coming to tell someone that they had done or were doing a good job. We created the index card exercise in that meeting. John did it and reviewed his results at the end of every day. By the end of the week, I was hearing comments from his employees such as, "Something has come over John—something major. It may have to do with religion. He's almost a different person. He even looks different."

Not all situations work out this well, but that one did. Attendance came under control, efficiency increased, and the employees were obviously pleased with the "new" John. My regret is that I didn't keep up with him over the years.

You CAN teach a chicken to dance if a) you're smarter than the chicken and b) it's worth the trouble. It comes back to cost (in terms of both time and money) and how much you are willing to pay for the changes you get. For example, there was a time when I was in need of an administrative assistant. The interviewing process was moving right along when a young lady came in who looked determined, and I knew that she was the one. When we discussed the opening, however, I found that she did not have a single skill that was specified in the ad. Not one! When I asked why she applied for the job even though she had no qualifications, she said, "I want to do better in life and I just know that I can do a good job."

It took the better part of an hour to discover a few reasons to hire her. She couldn't type, but she could print really well. She didn't know a thing about the use of a calculator although she could identify one by sight about two out of three attempts. She was raised in the boonies, meaning out in the country with no town in sight. When I asked where she lived, her answer was, "about three miles outside of Bean Station." The one thing she had that blew away the other applicants was one of the friendliest smiles that I had ever seen, and she showed it often. Also, she was very bright. I reasoned that it is much easier to teach a person to type than it is to teach them to be friendly.

I hired her and was never sorry for the decision. No one could have worked harder or made more progress. Cultural differences arose in the first week. She came into my office and asked to see the newspaper. The conversation went like this:

"Sure, which section would you like?"

"Obituaries," she said.

"Did someone you know die?"

"Yes, an old man who lived across the road from us."

"Was he sick?"

"No, he committed suicide." Sadness was written across her face.

"Oh my, did he have a problem with depression?"

"No, he thought that he had shot someone in the family."

"Huh?" I wasn't quite following her.

She patiently explained the story. "He got drunk and started shooting at his son. The son ran inside so the father put a few shots into the side of the house. They were yelling that someone was shot and I guess it must have upset him because he went down in the woods and either shot himself on purpose or by accident. We don't know which."

I was awestruck. "Did he shoot at people often?"

"Oh, yeah," she replied nonchalantly.

"It's a wonder no one was ever shot before."

"Who said that no one has ever been shot before?" she asked.

"Someone *has* been shot before?"

"Well," she pointed to her leg, "Look at this hole in my calf."

I studied the scar. "He shot you?"

"Yeah."

"I hope you called the sheriff and had this guy arrested!" By this time, I'm sure my expression was one of shock mixed with a little bit of fear.

"No, he didn't really mean to shoot me. He was actually shooting at my mother. He missed her and I got hit by the ricochet."

"He could have killed your mother?" My disbelief was growing. "Why in the world didn't you call the sheriff?"

"I would have if mom hadn't been shooting at him first," she clarified as she gave me one of her famous smiles.

Shortly afterward, she got her high school equivalency in two or three weeks' time, then started classes at the community college at night. From there, she went to the University of Tennessee and graduated with a degree in accounting. She married one of the salesmen in the company and is now an auditor for a large restaurant chain. I'm not making this up, and I am as proud of her as she is of herself. She did a lot of hard work. All I did was give her reason to believe that she was worth it by giving her a job and encouraging every small improvement she made along the way.

 **LEADER'S LAW: You don't always understand what other folks are accustomed to, but show patience and give them good reasons to work hard and you can help change a person's life for the better.**

FOUR

Nobody Learns to Juggle Without Dropping a Few Balls

'Tis a lesson you should heed,
Try, try again
If at first you don't succeed,
Try, try again.

William E. Hickson, 1870, Try and Try Again

So far, so good? If you have followed your directions for the index card assignment as described in Chapter Three, you are off to a very good start. You can probably already see a great change in terms of how people respond to you. We have a ways to go yet, but the rest is easy if you have people responding to you in a positive way. Some judgment is involved and mistakes will happen fairly often, but keep plugging. You probably won't make many mistakes and they will occur less and less frequently. Be warned that, occasionally, one of your comments might make a person feel very good and at another time the same comment to a different person might make that person want to smack you. Let's quickly try to illustrate.

For example, in the index card exercise from the last chapter, did every approving statement you made work out exactly as you expected? Did everyone respond to your comments exactly as you had planned? Probably not. Here are a few examples of responses following positive comments that have been reported to me.

"What are you after?"

"Go suck an egg."

"When does the other shoe drop?"

"Do I have to say something nice to you, now?"

These types of responses are not altogether uncommon, but they really don't happen that often. Most of the time, people actually appreciate positive comments. Some appreciate them, but are so unused to hearing them that they don't know how to show their appreciation. They just need to think about it for a little while and decide how to answer. STAY THE COURSE! The next time will almost always be better.

In many cases, saying positive things to others may be a new behavior for you, so you're not getting it exactly right. Try not to feel punished when this happens. You'll get it right the next time. I'm thinking of a guy who I used to know who surprised me with his tenacity. His name was Columbus Box and he was what we refer to in East Tennessee as a "sho 'nuf rounder." His long-suffering wife had to face a serious challenge every Friday. Friday was payday and she had to guess which one of three exits of the factory Columbus would use in leaving work. If she guessed right and rounded him off at the pass, the family would have a good week. If she guessed wrong, she had to find which beer joint he'd gone to and get there before all the money was gone.

When I say beer joint, I don't mean cocktail lounge. There's a big difference. Cocktail lounges are for somewhat orderly drinking. Beer joints are places where they serve the beer in long neck bottles and the waitress is named Spike. Fights are a nightly event to signal closing time.

One Monday morning, Columbus came to work and started doing something that no one would have ever suspected. He was passing out religious literature. Sometime over the weekend, he had been saved and loudly professed his acceptance of Jesus Christ as his personal savior. No one believed him and he took some verbal abuse from his fellow workers who thought he was just playing a joke. After a while, however, they had to admit that he was a changed man. His salty language disappeared and he went straight home every Friday night. Whenever the church doors opened, he was there, sitting on the front row. Yes, the man was definitely changed.

 **LEADER'S LAW: With a good enough reason, change can happen fast.**

One night they had a church meeting dedicated to a local family who had fallen upon hard times. The father hurt his back, the mother was sick, and the son was in jail. They needed help. The preacher began by saying in a very solemn tone, "I'd like to call on Brother Box to open with a word of prayer." If you've ever been called upon to pray in public, I'm sure you can remember the stress. If you've never been asked, you will probably have no problem in imagining how you might feel under those circumstances. The pressure was especially on in this church where the opening prayer was expected to last for several minutes. What could the reformed Brother Box do but give it a try?

He got off to a terrible start with a lot of stuttering and stammering. Then he had an idea. People who were there said that it was almost as though they saw a light come on inside his head. He decided that if he could ask for specific things, he could go on indefinitely. Heck, he might even raise his voice and get a little emotional. This was a turning point. Every sentence got louder as he said, "Oh Lord, deliver this family a barrel of flour. Oh Lord, deliver this family a barrel of corn meal. Oh Lord, deliver this family a barrel of sugar. Oh Lord, deliver this family a barrel of salt. Oh Lord, deliver this family a barrel of pepper." With that, he suddenly had a pained look on his face. He made a motion with his hand as if he were erasing a blackboard and said, "Naw, heck. That's too much pepper."

The congregation broke up in laughter and Columbus was almost sick with embarrassment. No one could have tried harder than he had. Unfortunately, he was just a little bit off. You'll be glad to know that the story does have a happy ending. Columbus shook it off and the next time he was called upon, he was ready and did a much better job.

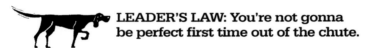 **LEADER'S LAW: You're not gonna be perfect first time out of the chute.**

We can learn through the mistakes of others and we can learn from their successes. Of course, good judgment is required before you start imitating the actions of others. It took a while for me to learn that what worked for someone else may not work for me. Know your own style and don't feel that you have to make any radical changes to be effective. Small changes usually do the job.

Years ago, I knew a man who was the manager of a large knitting operation. The equipment operators were 100 percent female, and he managed his department about as well as anyone I had seen. He was a chubby Irishman and the operators loved him. His approval was important to them and they would go far to get it. He spoke with an Irish brogue and called everyone "me darlin'."

When any one of them did something above and beyond, he would write the accomplishment down on an index card and tape a dime to it. Then he would walk to the operator's workstation while holding the card high above his head. It was amazing how quickly his walk gained the attention of everyone in the entire room. When he reached his destination, he would loudly sing the song *When Irish Eyes Are Smiling* (except he changed the words to *my irish eyes...*) with his beautiful tenor voice and then give her the card along with a big kiss on the cheek.

Everyone in the room would smile and applaud. He was good at creating strong reasons for his operators to perform well. Having said that about him, I will say this to you: DON'T TRY IT! You'll get your face slapped and you'll be charged with sexual harassment. You will probably be fired from your job, you may never work again, and I'll be surprised if anyone will ever again ask you to lunch. I recognized right away that while this means of appreciation was quite effective for this Irishman in this factory, it wouldn't work for *anyone* else.

Some people are very uncomfortable giving compliments if they have been slow to compliment in the past. It's a new behavior and in many ways it's like wearing a new pair of shoes. They will be a little stiff for a few days, but once they're broken in and become comfortable, we get a great deal of pleasure from them. The temptation at first is to slip the old ones back on for a little while.

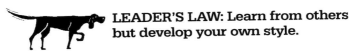 **LEADER'S LAW: Learn from others but develop your own style.**

I've been asked many times, "Isn't it true that in many cases, people like their compliments in reverse? Don't people feel good when someone uses sarcasm? If they smile, doesn't that mean that they like it?" My answer is, "Maybe, but probably not." Don Rickles was successful in building a career on his ability to insult people. It seems to have worked for him, but I don't think it would work for me. Such questions are usually asked by people who feel uncomfortable in saying approving things and would feel more comfortable in saying something insulting followed by a wink and a grin–which is intended to invalidate the sarcastic statement–and hope the performer assumes the opposite.

Does this actually happen? Sometimes. More often than not though, I've seen it backfire. The speaker walks away smiling at how well he showed his approval in a humorous way, but before he turns the corner, the performer grinds his teeth and says something that would not be taken well if it had been heard by the wrong person. Why take the chance? People are rarely insulted when their performance is sincerely complimented. Sometimes, our good intentions are not seen as clearly as we would like.

A different case of misguided intentions happened a few years ago at the University of Tennessee. Descriptions of this plan appeared in the newspaper and I would like to have had a closer look at them. Someone with the best of intentions decided that the football team needed more— here's that word again—*motivation*. Regardless of the fact that the previous year the team won ten games, someone sold the idea that they needed to get off to a better "running start" in the new season.

Here was the deal: If you win, you are treated like winners. If you lose, you will be treated like losers. Your post-game meal will not be steak and potatoes, but cheap hot dogs boiled in water with red dye dripping from them. This meal would be accompanied by a cold bun and a glass of Kool-Aid. There were other stipulations and consequences, but I don't recall what they were and for our purposes they are unimportant. Guess what? The team lost the first four games. Maybe five. (This happened years ago and I'm too lazy to look it up.) At any rate, Alabama came to town for a big game (as it always was). Tennessee lost that day, but in the locker room after the game, Coach Johnny Majors said something to the effect of, "Guys, you played well. I could not ask for more from you and I'm just sorry that you couldn't walk away with a win. You played like winners and you will be treated like winners. The steaks are on the grill. In fact, the losers' table is history. We'll have no more of that." They didn't lose another game for the rest of the season.

I have no hard data to prove the impact of the things that I have mentioned, and I would never try to have it published in a scientific journal. We don't know how many other important things were going on with the team at the same time. I believe, however, that it is a good example of how small things can have a major impact on performance. I believe, also, that it is a good example of how a well-meaning person can do the wrong thing even when it seems like a good idea at the time.

 **LEADER'S LAW: Don't let your good intentions fall to the wayside. Play the game well by building people up, not by breaking them down.**

FIVE

You Can't Apologize to a Dawg

If there's a way to do it wrong, he will.
Edward A. Murphy, Jr. 1949
Original quote later altered into the popular saying of
Murphy's law: "If anything can go wrong, it will."

Recently, I was having dinner with a friend. The friendship began when we were four or five years old. That made her my first friend, and our friendship has endured to this day. Since we don't have the opportunity to visit as often as we would like, our dinners tend to last for quite some time. Leadership has been on my mind lately so quite naturally the subject came up. She made the statement, "Isn't it true that some people just radiate leadership? I mean all they have to do is walk into the room and people fall in behind them."

Yeah, I'll concede that. It's a bit like going to the supermarket to buy a bar of soap. I know nothing about soap except that it should make bubbles and help me get clean. How do I go about making a choice? As I mentioned in Chapter One, I, and many other people, go for the soap that has the most attractive wrapper. The wrapper gets it into my cart. There will come a time, rather quickly in fact, when I want to see some bubbles. My great uncle Cicero once said, "Sometimes your prettiest bird dog can't hunt a damn lick." Consequently, even if you are in a nice wrapper, the time will always come when you have to stand and deliver. You have to practice what you preach.

As I said earlier, I am a dog kind of guy. I enjoy their company and I have always found them to be honest in everything they do. Bird dogs were very important where I grew up and they were the topic of many conversations. We didn't talk about a wide variety of topics. Farming was one. Politics was another if it was election time, and even then the incumbent usually enjoyed a serious advantage over the challenger who was not often taken seriously. However, people talked bird dogs year round.

Bird dogs were bought, sold, and traded in much the same way baseball players are traded today. If the dog cared, he never mentioned it. They were definitely important. A neighbor came by our house once to try and open negotiations for a dog we owned named Granny that happened to be my personal favorite. My dad said (I *think* it was a joke), "If you take Granny you'll have to take the boy, too." The neighbor didn't smile or blink. Then he asked, "How much does the boy eat?"

My enjoyment of hunting stayed with me even through college. In fact, my biggest problem in college was that I was missing the hunting season at home. When a friend of mine told me that his family was going to allow him to bring a bird dog to school for the season, I had mixed feelings. On the plus side, I would not miss the season that year. On the down side, if the dog was a good hunter, the family would never have let him go. Both of my feelings were right on target.

My college friend's dog was named Rathbone and he was the absolute worst. Many people don't know this, but the most shameful thing for a bird dog owner is when his dog points a rabbit. Word of such an incident travels fast and the owner will soon be the object of ridicule for several days. This is because bird dogs are rigidly trained not to point at rabbits. Rabbits are hunted by beagles, a breed considered much lower in the hunting world pecking order than bird dogs. When a bird dog points a rabbit, he (or she) demonstrates both a lack of training and a lack of self-discipline.

It soon became obvious why my friend's parents wanted Rathbone out of town for the season. Even a good dog may sometimes point a rabbit in damp or wet weather, but ole' Bone would do it in any kind of weather. One time when we were hunting on a damp day, he actually pointed at a mule. That was a new one on me, and it was a new low for bird dogs.

After the mule incident, we explained our problem to a friend, Buck, who happened to be an excellent trainer of bird dogs. Buck said, "Let me have him for a week and I'll bring you back a good dog." I had my doubts, but what did we have to lose? Even the quail were laughing at us. Buck returned the dog a week later and proclaimed him to be competent as long as we followed his directions which were as follows: If Rathbone should slip up and point a rabbit, do *not* shoot the rabbit or respond to it in any way. Do not punish the dog, because if he performs poorly, it's your fault. Take treats and carry them in your jacket pocket. When Rathbone does the job that he's supposed to do, give him a treat and pat him on the head.

We could hardly wait. The next day we went out and hadn't been hunting for more than five minutes when Rathbone pointed. We were thrilled until a bunny rabbit jumped out and tore across the field. My friend was furious. He laid down his shotgun, ripped a pine limb off a tree and proceeded to teach that stupid dog a lesson. When he swiped at the dog, he made a noise and about forty birds flushed all around us.

Naturally, we were startled. Neither one of us could get off a shot. We stood in silence for a while when my friend finally said, "Let's go call Buck and see if he knows a way to apologize to a dog." Unfortunately, there wasn't an apology that would repair Rathbone's hurt feelings and it was one of the least satisfying hunting seasons in my memory.

LEADER'S LAW: You can't undo what you've already done, so be careful or you may do some serious, even permanent, damage.

To a dog, actions definitely speak louder than words. They won't listen to logic and in case you haven't noticed, most people won't either. People may smile, nod, and give you assurances, but what counts is your behavior. Do you follow through? Do you always do what you say you're going to do? Do you show approval at every opportunity? People, like dogs, expect good things to happen when they do something good. When that doesn't happen, they do something else.

Dogs, as well as people, will welcome competent leadership. If they are disappointed in your performance, you will find that they have less and less time for you. If you are thinking that I'm saying that most people are only as intelligent as a dog, you are wrong, although dogs reach the average intelligence of a four- or five-year-old human child (as far as *we* know). But we humans and dogs have grown together as a species, and science has proven that we have similar behaviors (although ours are not as limited) when it comes to learning.

We do have one thing in common: the more competent the follower becomes, the more competence he or she expects from the leader. This lesson was driven home to me one time by a field-trial, champion hunting dog named Stonewall. I had never hunted with Stonewall before, though I had heard many stories about his skills and had always wanted to see him work firsthand. We didn't get off to a really good start. He just didn't seem that excited about hunting with someone he didn't know, but from all indications he was willing to give it a try.

Stonewall was one sharp dog. He knew what he was doing and it was a pleasure just to watch him work. When he pointed, it was as though he were posing for a picture. This is when I did the unforgivable and, as a result, our relationship, tenuous as it was, fell apart. When the birds flushed, I fired three shots and didn't so much as feather one.

Afterward, Stonewall turned slowly and glared at me for what seemed like an eternity. I had obviously wasted his precious time and talent. I could see it in his eyes.

After a long, awkward pause, I tried to apologize and explain to him that I had something in my eye, but it was obvious that he wasn't buying it. At long last, he turned and went back to work. He was looking for single birds now (since I had failed on the multiple-bird challenge) and he found one in short order. How could I possibly be ready? My stress level had increased by about 50 percent. I was totally intimidated by that dog. The bird quickly flushed again before I was ready and I missed again. This time Stonewall didn't even favor me with a glare. HE QUIT! He simply walked away and didn't stop until he got back to the truck. I wanted to talk with him and try to reach some level of understanding, but he wasn't interested in excuses. There was nothing that I could do other than take him back home.

Stonewall demanded competence. When he didn't get it at first, he allowed a second chance. When he still didn't get it, he was done. If he could have put it into words, and if he were generous, he would have said something along the lines of, "Thanks for the effort, but I think I'll wait for someone who knows how to support all of my efforts and hard work." It isn't difficult to think of comparable situations that happen with people. Without follow-through demonstrated by our leaders, we're nowhere and we may eventually give up, even if we stay. Stonewall had a choice. He didn't stay.

 **LEADER'S LAW: Luck helps, but you best develop your skills as a leader or you will eventually lose the talented employees who are willing and loyal enough to give you honest feedback and more than one chance.**

SIX

Who ARE
These People
Following Me?

If a man does not keep pace with his
companions, perhaps it is because he hears a
different drummer. Let him step to the music he
hears, however measured or far away

Henry David Thoreau, Conclusion in Walden, 1854

Leaders should always know as much as they can about their followers, so that their leadership strategies are on-target. A large group of people may engage in the same behavior and strive for a common goal, but the individuals in the group may have a wide variety of reasons for doing so. This might be a good place to examine some behaviors that seem odd to us until we discover or think that we have discovered a person's reasons for doing them.

One of my closest friends in this life was named Oscar. We met in the fifth grade when my dad decided that I should attend a city school where football was offered. (I was wide, don't you know.) Anyway, Oscar was the first person I met at the new school, and in the first minute of our meeting, he successfully relieved me of my lunch money. The strange thing is that I was *eager* to hand it over. In just a matter of seconds, Oscar had convinced me that he personally owned a Harley-Davidson motorcycle and that he would be riding it that very day if only he had some money for gas. He was only eleven years old, but also being eleven years old, I bought the story. I even insisted that he accept my lunch money. I figured that he could bring the Harley to school the next day and take me for a ride.

Oscar never brought the motorcycle to school, but he did take me for a ride and he did so regularly over the next fifty years. In fact, he was the most prolific liar I have ever known. Lying and scamming was just something he loved to do and he actually worked diligently to perfect his skills. Once (when I had grown to know him better), he told me that he sometimes spent hours in front of a mirror telling the most ridiculous lie he could come up with while maintaining a sincere expression on his face. That was probably a lie too, but that's what he said.

My favorite Oscar example took place at Bagley's Store. Bagley's was a kind of gathering place on slow days. People sat around on the porch, drank soft drinks, and discussed how badly everyone else's kids had turned out. One afternoon Oscar pulled in at the self-service pump and started gassing up his truck. One of the porch sitters called out, "Hey Oscar, come up here and tell us a lie." Does this sound like a challenge to you? It did to him.

He called back, "I ain't got time for that kind of foolishness today. A truckload of Georgia Bell peaches has turned over down at Eton Crossroads and the ditches on both sides of the road are waist deep in peaches as big as your fist. I'm going down there and load up."

Within seconds they all jumped off the porch, got into their trucks, and headed for Eton Crossroads. When Oscar had finished gassing up, he pulled his truck out of the way, came up on the porch, and bought a soft drink.

Mr. Bagley smiled and said, "They're gonna' be mad at you when they get back."

Oscar grinned, "I don't know why. They asked me to tell 'em a lie."

The interesting thing was that everyone knew about Oscar's proclivity to lie. Even so, more often than not, they believed his tales. The more ridiculous the lie, the more elated he was when someone believed it.

Oscar's reason for lying was the "thrill of victory" when he could get someone to believe a real whopper. Of course, the victory was not complete until the receivers eventually realized that they had been had.

 **LEADER'S LAW: People seek recognition in many ways, some in ways we will never understand.**

One point here is that some people are extremely difficult to lead. Oscar had a unique form of reinforcement and reward. It was the kind of reinforcement and reward that only he could deliver to himself. You can always find some way to influence any person if you discover some way to reinforce that person, but if an individual is already proud of their accomplishments and satisfied with who they are, it may take more time than you're willing to give to persuade that person to follow you.

 **LEADER'S LAW: Realize that what gets some people excited about doing things may be impossible for you to give them.**

One of the more interesting characters who would fit comfortably into this self-reinforcing category is Coot Green who was mentioned in Chapter Two. Coot was our town drunk and I must admit that he had his schedule worked out about as nicely as you could imagine. We had a few people in town who drank a great deal and wound up in jail quite often, but none had it going as smoothly as Coot. He was an umpire by trade and this turned out to be a wonderful selection of career paths, because it allowed him free time to pursue his other interests. The people of our town considered him to be a minor treasure. Everyone liked him. *I* liked him, and if *I* could like him, anybody could.

The reason I say this is because I was a catcher for our local baseball team and Coot spent a large part of the game hanging over my shoulder. He was always in demand as an umpire. He always called a good game, maintained control of the game, and he was the only one in town who had the umpire stuff: blue suit, mask, chest protector, and the little short-billed cap.

I only had a couple of small problems with Coot. During the hot months of baseball season in North Georgia, cool breezes are seriously absent. Coot's sweat must have been 100 proof. Even though I hadn't had anything stronger to drink than water, I would sometimes feel a bit giddy about midway through a game. Maybe it was my imagination. The second problem, though not serious, was that as the game began to get long, Coot's mind began to drift to visions of a cold beer in a frosty mug. After a while, every pitch was a strike. This provided a bit of an advantage to the home team because we had been through this before and knew to swing at every pitch because there would be no "base-on balls" after the fifth inning.

Since the fiasco with the elephant, Sheriff K. C. had enjoyed a fairly smooth ride until the day of the biggest baseball game of the season. We were playing Central Penny (Central High School sponsored by J. C. Penny Co.) from Chattanooga. Warm-ups were going fine until someone noticed that Coot hadn't shown up. Panic spread rapidly while people divided into groups to go look for him. We could have used another umpire, but this was Central Penny and we wanted everything to be just right. Coot, after all, was the only guy who had all the *stuff*.

Cooler heads prevailed as someone suggested that we check the jail first. He was there, of course. Panic rose to a new level when our coach learned that Coot was only in the third day of a ten-day sentence for drunk and disorderly conduct. (The sentence was unusually long since K. C. was trying to make it up to Coot for being turned out early during the episode with the elephant.) With coach's persuasion, that problem was solved in record time and Coot felt that he had reached a new level of importance. Obviously, he had. They let him out of jail long enough to call the game.

Coot was a man who felt proud of his accomplishments and was very comfortable and pleased with the person he had turned out to be. I did not personally hear the following conversation, but I am told that it happened and I believe it did. Waco Paul was a friend of Coot's and tried mightily to reach peer level with him. Coot, however, was the Roy Hobbs of town drunks and would never have a peer. Waco said, "Coot, it is my opinion that you are the best town drunk there ever was."

Coot replied, "It's a gift."

LEADER'S LAW: There is always somebody who wants to be recognized as the best, even if it is the best complainer, the best at throwin' a cold blanket on a good idea, the best at doing just enough to get by, the best at being down-right unforgiving . . . these are the toughest people to inspire.

However, if you can find something positive they do and recognize them for that, you're on your way, because people do more of what they are rewarded for.

SEVEN

Football –
a Southern Religion

Trust men and they will be true to you;
treat them greatly and they will show
themselves great.

Ralph Waldo Emerson

Since this is a book that is largely dependent upon the
Southern experience, I thought it only appropriate that I
add a bit on football and the leaders (good and bad) who
have been part of the scene for so many years. College
football in the South is actually more religion than sport.
Saturday is considered a holy day of obligation when people come together to have their emotions elevated or shat-
tered, depending upon whose group of teenagers scored
more points over the course of a three-hour event. I don't
know how it came to be that way or how it got to be so
doggone important, but there it is and you go with what
you got.

All of my life I have heard that football builds character, leadership, responsibility, and so on, but to be honest, I have seen it go both ways. Your long-term leaders, all-around fine people, and generally worthless people seem to take part in about the same mix whether they are in the Glee Club, 4-H Club, or the marching band. All are worthy activities that should go into the plus column of our own personal history books and leadership can be developed in all of them. The major difference is in the size of the audience. Let's face it. Not many people are going to show up to see your prize calf, but it seems that everyone in town shows up to see a football game. The point is that leadership and character are not a matter of which club you're in, but are determined by how you participate as a member of the team you're on.

 **LEADER'S LAW: Don't be overly influenced by an impressive list of "I belonged to this" because prestigious titles don't always equal honorable activity.**

My dad worked with a gentleman named Jude Anderson and when I was born, he told my dad, "Give that boy all the milk he can drink and he'll save you $1,000 a year some day." That was the cost of college in those days and it had worked for Jude, since his son Alf had gone to the University of Georgia on a football scholarship. Years later, my dad said that I drank far more milk than could be covered by $1,000 a year and if the cost of college hadn't gone up so fast he never would have come out on the deal. (I earned a full athletic scholarship to the University of Georgia.) Alf was my high school coach and I still think of him as one of the finest men that I have ever known.

When I turned eleven years of age, my dad took stock of his long-term plan and decided that it was working. I was as wide as an armoire. However, as I alluded to before in the story of how I met Oscar, my father had failed to notice that football was not offered as a sport option in county schools. We only had basketball since that was the only sport that could be covered by our athletic budget. We had six uniforms and I was not a contender for any of them, even if there had been one in my size. Therefore, I was transferred to a city school and endured a long six-mile commute for the rest of my school days. This was the first link in a chain of events that dramatically changed my life.

Allow me to describe the most miserable day in my life up to that point.

It was August in North Georgia. The weather was hot and humid with no breeze and no shade, and in case you've never been in Georgia in the summer, think of sitting in the hottest sauna available while fully dressed. It was the first day of football practice.

1) I didn't know a single person.
2) My uniform was too big (even after all that milk).
3) The field was comprised of dirt and dead grass, a large amount of which had found its way into my pants forming an indescribable itchy concoction.
4) The coach had involved me in a full-speed scrimmage and his only instruction was, "When you see somebody holding and/or running with the ball, knock his ass down."

Why would I want to do that? I thought. It would surely be painful for all involved. Can you imagine how I was feeling at the time? Why had my dad done this to me?

Then it happened. I looked up to see a big older kid running my way and carrying the ball under his arm. This called for a very big decision on my part. Should I follow my coach's direction or get out of the way? This was an easy choice to make as far as I was concerned—get out of the way. The next decision was where do I go to get out of the way? If I moved, I might run into somebody and get hurt if they decided to go in the same direction. Things were moving very fast and my life flashed before my eyes. I decided to stand still and let the big guy go where he pleased. Maybe I could even kinda' wave at him as he ran by and save a little bit of face in the process via humor. Since the big kid decided that it would please him to run directly over me, all of my quick-witted planning went to waste.

Because I had made the wrong choice in meeting my goal of self-protection, we collided and the ball must have gone ten feet in the air. The first part of my body to hit the ground was the back of my head and it went down-hill from there (not my head, the situation). I was about to make a bad day even worse because I knew that I was going to cry in a manner that was far noisier than normal. That's when the big event happened. The coach ran up to my crumpled body and before I could work up a good cry, he grabbed my face guard, lifted me (at what seemed at the time) above his head and yelled, "Did everybody see that? That's what we want to see out here. Keep your eye on this guy. He's a very dangerous person!"

Do you think I cried then? No, I actually smiled. The whole day turned around and all I had to do was stand there (for as long as I could, at least). I quickly forgot the pain and like Junior, my snake-hunting yard dog, I had a new mission in life. I had a reason to go out and seek people who were holding and/or running with footballs. I enthusiastically pursued this mission for many years.

 **LEADER'S LAW: Even less-than-enjoyable jobs and duties can be fulfilling, even joyful, when the right consequences exist.**

During high school, I was recruited by a few colleges and enjoyed weekend visits to complementary football games and campus tours with all the fixins'. The University of Alabama was one college that recruited me and, of course, I scheduled a visit. The coach was a guy named Ears Whitworth and I had heard some horror stories about him (mostly from recruiters of other colleges). I met him and spent a little time with him and he seemed like a nice enough guy. However, I did not ride into town on a truckload of cabbage and realized that since he was in a selling mode, of course he would be nice. Determined not to be fooled by insincere kindness, I signed up with the University of Georgia. During the spring of my freshman year at Georgia, Alabama fired Coach Whitworth and replaced him with Bear Bryant. Guess who showed up as a Georgia assistant coach? You got it. It was Ears. He turned out to be one of the finest coaches that I've ever had, and he provided one of the finest examples of leadership that I had seen up to that time. He always knew what to do and when to do it. When you needed a reason to reach down and go a little harder, he gave you a reason—and in a positive way. He seemed to know when enthusiasm was on the wane and he always did something to turn it around.

One day when everyone was tired and cranky and fights were breaking out every five minutes, he called a time out. He walked up and put his arm around a guy we all called Preacher. We called him that because that is what he was. He actually delivered the sermon from time to time in an Athens church. He was a fine person and a wonderful football player on offense. Defense was another story entirely. Since this was a time when the NCAA had changed the rules and made it necessary for every team member to play both offense and defense, his defensive weakness made it difficult for him to log very much playing time. (This system went on for ten or twelve years before the NCAA wised up and went back to the two platoon system.) Preacher played fullback on offense and attempted to play linebacker on defense.

Anyway, Coach Whitworth said "Preacher, do you mind if I call you *Preacher?*" The answer, of course, was "No, sir." Then he said, "Well good. I do admire a man with religious convictions. I'm a religious person myself. Yes sir. I go to church every Sunday and I pray every night. So far, my prayers haven't been answered, but I'm going to stay at it. What I pray for shouldn't be too much to ask. I say, 'Oh Lord, won't you please deliver to me a mean sumbitch that can play linebacker.'"

It took about ten minutes for everyone to quit laughing. Was it time wasted? No way. When we went back to work, spirits were high and everyone was more productive, including Preacher.

I ran into Coach Whitworth one Saturday night while I was involved in flagrant disregard of team training rules. If he ever got angry, he never showed it. This night, he walked up and put his arm around me and said, "Porky, these are the best years of your life. Football is your job and it will be gone soon enough. Your education is the thing that you will keep forever and your social activities you'll remember for the rest of your days. That's why I'm glad to see that you're taking full advantage of your opportunities. You just need to remember one thing. When you get caught dancing, you gotta pay the fiddler." A few days later, with the extra wind sprints the coach gave me, I was thinking that either this was one overpaid fiddler or I should have done a lot more dancing.

What is a good coach, anyway? Is it a person with a great win/loss record? A win/loss record is certainly accepted as an indicator of a good coach, but in my opinion, there's more to it than that. Is it a coach's ability to turn bad football players into good ones? If that had been our measuring stick, many would agree that, in my case, they were all miserable failures. So what is it? In my opinion, a good coach is a person who can provide good reasons for performing at your best.

Quinton Lumpkin was a coach at the University of Georgia and he was the most physically intimidating man that I have ever been around. If he said "Do it!" you did it—no questions asked. People pushed themselves far to gain his approval and pushed themselves even further to avoid disappointing him.

One day at practice, we were doing one-on-one drills which consisted of one man blocking another. Coach Lumpkin told the blocker which direction to take the defender. When I looked up, there stood Big Bob. He stood about six foot five and weighed around 300 pounds. His advantage over me was about eight inches and 100 pounds. That was big. These days, some schools have teams where the players *average* that size, but in those days, he was a giant freak. Before the play, Coach Lumpkin took me aside, rubbed his chin and said, "I hope I don't hurt your feelings, but I don't think you have a prayer of blocking Bob. Tell you what. When I call the snap, don't bother trying to block him. Instead, take one step back and unload a fist right to his chin. It's gonna make him really mad, so give him all you've got. Don't worry. I'm in this with you." I have to admit that I was extremely apprehensive about doing this, but never for one second considered not doing it. When I did it, Bob, of course, didn't see one bit of humor in it. I walked away knowing what it must feel like to have a building fall on you. As good as his word, Coach Lumpkin was there to help.

I had other good coaches, of course, and a lot of really bad ones too. It's easy to remember the good ones because they gave everyone something that they could take along and use for the rest of their lives. To be honest, I have a hard time recalling the names of the bad ones and that is as it should be. Their influence was as temporary as the game that we were called together to play.

In later years, I was introduced to a gentleman and when he heard my name he said, "By golly, I remember when you played football at Georgia." My response was, "Wow! That's impressive. I can barely remember those years myself." The truth is I don't have a crystal clear memory of those years. Maybe I have only just so much space for memories and most of that is taken up by the fine group of men who have influenced my life: Alf Anderson, Quinton Lumpkin, Ears Whitworth, and Jim Whatley. They are all gone now. They didn't create a football star, but they made me want to be a better man and that's what it's all about.

 **LEADER'S LAW: People usually remember and follow the advice of leaders who guided them in positive ways and supported them in good times and bad.**

When it comes to football, one of my favorite quotes came from the father of Dan Morino. Before a big game, the senior Morino was asked about the very intense pressure that his son must be feeling as the game grew near. His response was, "Pressure? Pressure is when you get laid off at the mill and you've got a wife and six kids at home who have to eat. Football's just a game."

EIGHT

When You're Not in Kansas Anymore

Every man is said to have
his peculiar ambition.

Abraham Lincoln

Most of us will always encounter times when we are called into a different environment and find ourselves confused because we haven't taken the time to do a little bit of research. Before entering a new situation, or trying a new approach to leadership, you may need to do a bit of investigating in terms of the things that people expect, the local jargon, and things that people typically like or dislike. You probably won't need to go to the library and do a great deal of reading, but you should at least talk with someone who has been there. Also, you don't have to go to the other side of the world to find new environments. They are often right next door. You'd be surprised, for example, at the problems I faced when my barber lost his lease.

He had been cutting my hair for many years and I suppose that I expected him to be available for as long as I needed him. You see, he decided that the loss of his lease was a sign from a higher source that he should retire. This left me in need of a new barber, although the problem was not pressing since at the time I only had my hair cut about every six to eight weeks. Consequently, when my barber first retired, I was in no big rush to find a replacement. Then one day I looked into the mirror and suddenly (it always seems to creep up on me) I drastically needed a haircut. In times of crisis, I tend to go to my wife first for a solution and this time as she usually does, she came through with an answer. She suggested that the lady who cuts her hair could do a wonderful job on mine. Goodbye barber shop and hello unisex salon. I should have better prepared myself for what to expect.

The first thing my new hairdresser said was, "Step this way and we'll give you a shampoo." I tried to explain that I wash my hair every morning and had done it that day no more than a couple of hours ago. She wasn't having any of that. I apparently needed another one right then. When she finished, I had to walk a considerable distance through a large group of ladies in various stages of hair design with my own hair wet and standing in more directions than a punk rocker.

As the process continued, she asked, "Would you like a little mousse?" When I regained my composure, I said, "No, I don't think so. I travel a lot, you see, and I don't even have time to take proper care of a dog. I don't think a moose would work out at all." She looked at me like I was a fool.

There were several problems to be dealt with that day and I'm afraid that I did a poor job of it. When we left, my wife was embarrassed, I was embarrassed, they charged me $20; and, in my opinion, I still needed a haircut. This was a very frustrating experience and was getting to be more so every day.

A week later, I noticed a sign that read, "Barber Shop—Downstairs." It was under the drug store and I felt right at home when I walked through the door. There were two chairs; each one had a barber sitting in it reading the newspaper and watching a soap opera on television. They were discussing what Victor's reaction would be when he discovered that the sperm bank had been robbed of one of his deposits and that he was now a father again. I joined in on the discussion and we decided that he probably would not find out for several more years. My new barber gave me the best haircut I have ever had and charged me $10. Even though he didn't offer me a moose, he gave me his best guess regarding who set fire to the Abbott's pool house.

 **LEADERSHIP LESSON: When you don't do your homework, you make more work for yourself than is necessary.**

Granted, even when you do the preliminary work, you may run into problems. I contracted some work in Morocco a few years ago and since it seemed to be a whole different culture, I felt that the wise thing to do was to examine the mores and folkways (Sociology 101. Dr. Belcher would be proud) of the country beforehand. My investigation wasn't nearly thorough enough, but I managed to stay out of trouble for the most part. However, I did discover that the Moroccan lifestyle wasn't just different from that of America. It was *WAY* different. Small things kept coming up. For example, I had read that most social activity includes only males. This didn't bother me in the least. I wondered where the women went, but it was no big deal. I supposed that they simply stayed at home with the children and any other wives the husband might have. One thing that was definitely not in the literature was the fact that men commonly hold hands when they are sitting together or walking together. This was somewhat interesting although it was truly no big deal to me . . . at least, not for a few days. That's when they started wanting to hold hands with *me*.

I made several good friends while I was there and all of them wanted to hold hands. I spent a lot of time standing around with my hands in my pockets and driving with both hands on the wheel. No one seemed to notice my reluctance to hold hands and they seemed oblivious to my sometime extreme avoidance behavior. Yet, they never gave up and although I've never admitted it until now, they eventually wore me down. After a while, I finally said, "What the hell. If you want to hold hands, grab on." That was the limit, though. I was firm in my mind that I would go absolutely no further. I was relieved to learn that no one wanted to do anything more than that and they could hold hands for hours on end. I never became completely comfortable with it, but it was somewhat bearable.

In my preparation, my colleagues who had been to Morocco before me shared a great deal of useful information. In general, people there receive little or no praise. They just don't do that. This was not bad news to me. I happen to know that praise and demonstrations of approval make people happy, make people exert more effort, and generally make people try harder. Also, people are drawn to the source of approval, which in this case, I hoped would be me.

My job was to train the lower and middle operations managers of a textile plant. Most of them had never worked a day in their lives at such work (no problem) and none of them could speak English. Language, however, should be no great problem I reasoned because I had taken French in high school and felt moderately equipped to handle whatever might arise.

When I arrived in Morocco, I was completely on my own and it quickly became apparent that these people did not understand French nearly as well as I had expected. The other students in my high school French class had understood me just fine. These people only giggled and looked embarrassed for me. Where did they learn this language, anyway?

Luckily, I had no problem placing food orders in restaurants, although when my food arrived I was always surprised to see what I had asked for. To fit in, I always ate it, but I rarely knew what it was. Naturally, this made me feel a bit apprehensive. I had only a few days before I was to meet my young managers and up to this point the only thing that I had been able to do without much fanfare was buy a ballpoint pen.

When the day arrived and I had my young managers together, I was really surprised to see just how young they really were. They looked like children and it was discouraging to find that they didn't speak French any better than the rest of the people I had met. My number-one priority, though, was to notice the good things that they did and demonstrate my approval as often as possible. Even I was surprised at how smoothly everything went.

As you probably know, training animals is not difficult if you know how to show approval and reward behavior. Don't get me wrong, I'm not calling the Moroccans animals, but all of us in the human race are still in the animal kingdom and we respond in much the same way as most mammals on the food chain. If people have lived a life with very little approval, it should not be surprising how quickly they bond to someone who supplies it in abundance. They loved me and I've never worked with a group of people who tried any harder. It was very easy to love them right back. In fact, they turned out to be my most favorite group of all time. I hated to leave them, but I felt really good about the things that we had accomplished and I was confident of their preparation.

I had one week left and all I had to do was write my final report. A new friend of mine who was assigned to the American Embassy in Rabat had offered me the use of an oceanfront villa for the rest of my stay and I was looking forward to it. I wrote the report in two days and I was getting into some serious relaxation when a messenger came and asked me to call the office. The office was a department of the Moroccan government that was responsible for the project. This didn't sound good, not good at all.

As it turned out, the managers (*my* managers at the textile factory) had gone on strike. I was terrified, wondering what I had done to cause such a thing. Do they kill people for this? I wondered. When I reached the office, it was obvious that they were plenty upset. The director spoke poor English and I was beginning to accept the fact that my best French was not as adequate as I had believed it to be early on. Through poor language skills and sign language, I finally understood what had happened.

The mill managers had been asked to help erect the new machinery that was beginning to arrive from Germany. They reasoned that since they were in management, actual physical work was beneath them. They were insulted and responded to the request by calling an immediate strike. How, I wanted to know, could I be responsible for this? After we struggled with the language for a while and played charades for a while longer, the answer I received was, "You did not cause the strike. You are to fix it. They want you to come and resolve the conflict." So much for my seaside resort.

They loaded me into the back seat of a government car and started the four-hour trip to the plant site. During the whole trip I thought, what can I possibly say to them to make them *want* to go back to work? I had four hours to come up with a persuasive argument. I need not have worried.

As soon as we got there, I took one of the guys aside and asked what was going on. Basically, his answer was, "The strike was a knee-jerk reaction. We should not have done it. Since we did, however, someone needs to give us a reason to back down from our position and go back to work. That will be you, Sir." Suddenly, there was no problem. My real task was to help the managers save face. Anything I said would be accepted as an adequate reason to go back to work. I'd be a hero. I began wondering if I could change my travel arrangements when the King sent me an invitation to dinner. The reason that I presented was unimportant. They barely let me finish before they ran out the door and went back to work erecting machines. I could hardly wait to see what the government was going to do for me in return for my good deed.

I got a free ride back to Rabat. That was nice. No one bothered me for the next three days while I chilled out in my borrowed villa and got ready to go home. That was it. It was Morocco, after all, and they don't do a great deal of rewarding. I should have remembered that from the research.

 **LEADER'S LAW: It is not difficult to change the behavior of others. Sometimes we can even it do it unintentionally and without trying, which is also why we should pay close attention to what we do and say.**

 **LEADER'S LAW: The effects of recognition and reward are universal among human beings, no matter what their language or culture.**

NINE

Funny, You Don't Look Otherish

I want to do it because I want to do it.

Amelia Earhart

After more than thirty years of conducting workshops and seminars, you might think that stage fright would be a thing of the past for me. It isn't and I don't think it ever will be. Typically, it begins the night before I'm to make a public appearance and by breakfast I'm as tight as a banjo string. This feeling normally continues for about the first twenty or thirty minutes of the workshop. Then the workshop starts to be fun.

A senior colleague and friend, Courtney Mills (don't make fun of his name; he was in the Airborne), and I were once doing simultaneous workshops in the same building in Minnesota. It's always a pleasure to travel with Courtney. I enjoy his company and his conversation, which is always honest and open. Anyway, it was surprising to hear him say that he is always nervous before a workshop. Same as me! We didn't discuss it very much. We both know why we're nervous and we both know how much more difficult it was thirty years ago when we first started our careers.

Actually, conducting my first workshop was one of the worst experiences of my life. The only thing that kept me from fleeing at the time was the fact that I didn't have any place to go. The participants conspired to make me miserable and they did one fine job of it.

After it was announced that the workshop would be conducted in a series of weekly meetings, they all agreed that they didn't have time for such interruption. Next they brainstormed ways that they might put an end to my workshop as quickly as possible. They came up with a wonderful plan. "Let's kill his spirit," someone suggested.

"How do we do it?"

"Nobody speaks. Nobody moves. Nobody laughs or smiles. To the extent that it is possible, we are made of stone." It was the ultimate in diabolical schemes. I had never known such suffering before that day.

I made several phone calls to my manager and co-workers and asked everyone, "What do I do?" No one really had an answer. The only response I received was, "Why not read the class text and try to practice what you preach?"

What kind of stupid advice is that? It was, however, the only advice that was offered and I was forced to go with it for the lack of anything better. The advice turned out to be good.

I went to the bank and bought ten silver dollars. The plan was to give one to anyone who made a sound. A burp or a sneeze would be enough. Anything would be a start. About ten minutes into the session, someone mumbled. It was very weak, but worth a follow-up. I turned to the class and asked, "I'm sorry. Did somebody say something?" There was nothing but silence. "Come on now." More silence. I waited. Finally, someone said, "It was me." I smiled and said, "Please repeat it so we can address it." He seemed to take a deep breath and then said, "I think all this stuff about recognition and reward improving performance is a bunch of bullshit." As you can imagine, this was fairly disappointing for a first comment. It did, however, meet the "sound" criteria and I thanked the man and handed him the silver dollar. He looked rather puzzled as he asked, "What's this for?" I answered, "It's for making a comment. I want questions and comments and you just gave me one. Thank you." Another hand went up. When I recognized the supervisor of the facility, he said, "I think it's a bunch of bullshit too." My response was, "Sorry, we'll need a different comment this time." That was it. The ice melted immediately and there was more conversation back and forth than I actually needed for the duration of the project.

The next crisis occurred a year or so later when, on a follow-up visit, I discovered that the bank stopped selling silver dollars. I passed them out only rarely by that time, but going in without a few in my pocket would be very uncomfortable. It was a bit like driving your car on a trip and knowing that you don't have a spare tire in the back. The tires are good, but still . . . I need not have worried, because I no longer needed the silver dollars to encourage participation.

The next event that changed my life happened in a workshop that I was attending rather than conducting. The instructor was fairly skilled and he made several good points even though I can remember only one of them. The point has stuck because I had an opportunity to try it out early on and the results were so good that I have continued to use it to this day. He said, "Be 'otherish.' People take the time and spend their money to sit in front of you to be helped. They want information that they can use. Your gestures and style of delivery are important only if they help a person learn."

His advice may not sound like a big thing to you. You may have that point in mind all day long every day. Yet, this advice caused a big change in the way I respond to people in every situation, not just workshops. If you want to be helpful to others, others will want to be helpful to you. Be otherish.

This does not relieve all stress, but it relieves the big ones. Pre-workshop stress, as referenced in the beginning of this chapter, is light and of short duration. Granted, being otherish won't make people happy when the air conditioning is broken or they've been asked to reschedule their vacation in order to attend, but hey, a little stress is good for you.

In an earlier chapter, I offered a definition of leadership as getting things done through others. Here's a second definition that I like even better: *leadership is making those around you successful.* This definition tends to give a great deal more importance to the term *otherish.* True leaders want people around them to succeed. That is the true measure of a leader's success.

In the week before I left for college, my dad sat me down to listen to some advice. This is something that he rarely did and I was interested in his offering of wisdom. He said, "You're reaching an age when you will be seriously evaluating young ladies as long-term partners in life. You may make that selection while you're in school. All other things being equal go for the one with the most money." My darlin' Becky had lost her rich Great Aunt just a few years before and I was told that she had been affectionately remembered in her will. I found out later that her inheritance was two pieces of cut glass and a fiddle. We still have the cut glass. I traded the fiddle for a banjo and we still have that too. Since all other things were not equal, money never came into it anyway. She was then and remains to this day, the most otherish person I've had the pleasure of being around.

The state of Tennessee has recently initiated a *star rating* system whereby all child care facilities are rated for quality of care. Becky's job is to visit the facilities in an eight-county area (usually at their request) and advise them of things that need to be done to improve their evaluation when it occurs. When she does this, an interesting thing happens. She actually becomes, at least emotionally, a part of the organization that she is trying to help. Sleeves are rolled up, physical labor is expended, and she sweats out the evaluation as though she owned the place. When they achieve a maximum rating, she celebrates. When they don't, she frets for a while and then starts making plans for what they need to do before the next evaluation. It is important to her that they succeed, and most of the time, they do.

Can being otherish be taken too far? That would be an individual call. Becky, for example, provides everyone with all her phone numbers including our home phone. She encourages her clients to call whenever they have questions or problems that need to be addressed, and they do. Do they ever! Because of her otherishness a sort of bonding takes place and people want to share good news and bad news with her without delay. They call with ideas that they would like to try, and they call to ask questions about changes that didn't work out when they attempted them. Her approval is important to them and when they deserve it she gives it without reservation. People need approval and validation and these people have a readily available source which is limited only by a busy signal. The demand for her time and attention is rarely a problem for her.

My dad gave me one more bit of advice that has been

very valuable to me and I passed it on to my son when he left home. He said, "When you and your wife are deciding what kind of work to do, don't let money be the sole criteria. Choose something that you enjoy doing. The money will be there and you'll never work a day in your life." I haven't hit a lick in over thirty years. I don't think Becky has either.

Fat Grigsby was a guy who certainly subscribed to being otherish and choosing an enjoyable way of making a living. He was a bootlegger in my area and he really felt that since the nearest legal whiskey was as far away as Chattanooga, he was obliged to serve his fellow man by making it more conveniently available. It was more than twenty-five miles of crooked road to Chattanooga and he wanted to save his thirsty friends from having to take the risky trip. This, I think, was otherish, especially true if the traveler had a tendency to quench his thirst before he started back from the long trip.

Fat was of the opinion that while the concept of working in the conventional sense was a noble theory, it was a shaky way to make a living in practice and he wanted no part of it. I know that I've never heard of him working except in helping his fellow man avoid that hazardous trip to Chattanooga. He was dedicated to that, though. He even came up with a creative way to make sure that his product was convenient for his customers. He opened a restaurant and named it The Slab Side Inn.

There was nothing in the kitchen but whiskey and one of those big steel spoons. That spoon must have been two feet long. He also had a gallon can of catsup. The Slab Side Inn was in almost every respect a liquor store. Every once in a while, a stranger or a serious Baptist would walk in and order food. This presented no major problem since the alley that ran behind his place separated his back door from the back door of the Oakwood Café. He would yell the order across the alley and the cook at the Oakwood would prepare it and yell back. Fat would then fetch the order and deliver it to the customer. It worked quite well . . . for a while.

While everyone in the area accepted Fat's enterprise as one of public service, agents of the U. S. Treasury Department, commonly known as *revenuers,* took an almost opposite view. They raided his café and Fat subsequently did a little time. He was actually philosophical about the whole thing. He said, "Hey, they got to make a living too." The only thing that bothered him was why moonshine was illegal in the first place.

I think he must have given up bootlegging after that. If he ever did it again, I never heard about it. From then on, he restricted his activities to gambling. His philosophy of life was exemplified by an encounter he had with a guy who was trying to sell him a watch. The guy wanted to know how a man without a watch could turn down such a good deal. Fat replied, "When I get tired of sleeping, I get up. When I get hungry, I eat. When I get bored, I look for a card game. When I get tired, I go home and go to bed. I ain't ketchin' no planes, trains, or busses, so what do I need with a damn watch?"

The guy blinked his eyes and looked around for a minute or two and then he spoke. "Does anybody else need a watch?"

 **LEADER'S LAW: Life's too short to spend it being unhappy. Either change the job or change jobs!**

TEN

Creativity
May be
Overrated

We all live under the same sky,
but we don't all have the same horizon.

Konrad Adenauer

I admire creative people. They tend to put forth a lot of good ideas, refine the ideas of others, and keep me supplied with ideas that I can apply and use as my very own. Most people view creativity as a desirable quality and many try to develop their own skill at creating. Some can and some can't. To those who can and do, I will use this opportunity to say, "Thank you. You have made life easier for me." To those of you who can't, I will say, "Do not despair." Many people go through life without having a great number of creative thoughts. Many of them have been very successful leaders.

How many truly original thoughts are left, anyway? This earth is old now and it's been covered with people for quite a long time. In the beginning, there must have been original thoughts popping up every day. Today, however, we most frequently take the thoughts of others and put our own twist on them, refine them, tighten them up a little, and hopefully improve them. That's what it's all about. People keep looking for a better way.

We learn from the movies that every great detective has to have a "straight man." In most cases, the brilliant detective would never have solved a crime without the innocent comments made by the straight man. Sherlock Holmes had Dr. Watson, Charlie Chan had Number One Son, and Nick Charles had his wife Nora. You know how it works. The straight man says, "Tomorrow is Mother's Day." The detective says, "Say that again." The straight man dutifully repeats, "Tomorrow is Mother's Day." The detective then snaps his fingers and says, "Of course! That's it! That's what I've been missing! Get the car Straight Man; we have to prevent a murder."

Straight men come in all kinds of shapes and sizes, but where would we be without them? How do you suppose Sir Isaac Newton came up with the Law of Gravity? I don't really know, of course, but I'm thinking that he probably came up with it quite by accident. His wife probably said something like, "Ike, if you drop another coffee cup our inventory of crockery will become gravely low." To this, he scratched his chin and replied, "What did you just say?" She stared at him and repeated herself very firmly.

"Hon," he grinned knowingly, "We may just have something here." "What?" she asked.

"Why, the Law of Gravity of course."

"What?" she said tiredly.

"Yes . . . that's what I'll call it, the Law of Gravity!"

She probably pointed her finger in his chest and shouted, "Is that it? Is this your big breakthrough? Any fool knows that if you keep dropping our dishes we will eventually run out of them."

"Good point." He started scratching his chin again. "Give me a little time to work on it."

Of course, the rest is history.

 **LEADER'S LAW: Creative people also need the types of people who can help them implement and enable their ideas, so recognize the value of everyone's contributions.**

My Great Uncle Willie, on the other hand, at least from my observation, never had a creative thought in his life. Well, maybe he did way back there someplace. He's considerably older than I and perhaps he had several creative ideas before I was born. I don't know. I do know that he was one of the original employees of the Oak Ridge National Laboratories during World War II and played a part in the creation of the atom bomb. He wasn't a scientist, but he worked in the commissary, lived in the dormitory that was provided by the government, and through his efforts he probably shortened the war by several weeks. I do know that he was a man who carefully guarded his routine. He did the same things over and over on a regular basis and that, I've read someplace, contributes to a long life (or maybe it only seems like a long life).

Every night, Uncle Willie bought a case of beer to take back to his dormitory room. Then he would drink it. He did not have a refrigerator so we assume that he either drank very rapidly or cultivated a taste for warm beer. He never drank anything stronger than beer during the week. In keeping with his routine, we always looked forward to his visiting the family once every month. Even in this, he never varied from his routine.

Here are the steps:

1) Take a taxi to the Knoxville bus station.
2) Buy a bus ticket from Knoxville to Dalton, Georgia.
3) Be expelled from the bus in Chattanooga for inappropriate behavior.
4) Call someone in Dalton to come and get him in Chattanooga.
5) Hire a taxi to take him back to Oak Ridge on Sunday afternoon.

Then the cycle would start all over. He lived longer than all his brothers and sisters and I believe routine and lack of stress were the contributing factors. All the kids loved him because another significant part of his routine was giving each of us a half-dollar. We always tried to get to him early so that we could come back later and maybe convince him that he hadn't done it yet and he would give us all another one. Please excuse my digression. Let's get on with creativity.

In the last chapter, I told you about giving a silver dollar to a man for his unacceptable comment. About twenty years later, I used the example in an Advanced Performance Management workshop. Courtney Mills, consultant, and I were co-instructors. At the break, Courtney came up to me and said that although the story actually happened to him, I was perfectly welcome to use it whenever I felt that it would be appropriate or useful.

Give me a break! It happened to *ME* and my theory is he liked the example so much that he decided to put his own spin on it and use it as his own. Now he has used the story for so long that he really thinks it happened to him! He has the same theory about me, of course. The point is that one of us borrowed it from the other and made it our own. I'm either thankful or flattered and it doesn't really matter which. We learn from the mistakes of others and we also learn from their successes. Given a choice, I choose to take my lessons from among the things that worked rather than those that did not. If something worked for someone else, chances are that it will work for me too. I'll help myself and urge you to do the same—giving credit when credit is due, of course.

I'm thinking of a most interesting example of creativity that actually borders on original. Pudlo Springfield was, in some ways, a dadgum genius. There was never a radio so broken that he couldn't fix it. The same was true of television sets. The creativity came in his approach to the enterprise. He was actually the first door-to-door repairman that I ever heard of. He didn't own a car so he carried his tools in his pockets and walked everywhere he went. Of course, there weren't very many tools. He had a pair of pliers and a few screwdrivers of various sizes, but you would definitely have to say that Pudlo traveled light. If parts were needed, as they usually were, he would tell the customer where to go and what to get while he waited. He would say something like, "Run down to the Western Auto Store and get me an O-Z4 and a buffer condenser. A cold drink would be nice while I wait for you to get back." When I got back, he would complete the job and then discuss the bill with my mother. This was the most creative part of all.

He'd say, "Well now let's see. I need 30¢ for a pack of cigarettes. I just ran out of mayonnaise, so that will probably be about 70¢. This afternoon, I need to go to Cleveland and I think the bus fare is $1.40. That brings your bill to $2.40." I suppose we were lucky that he never came by needing a suit of clothes for a wedding scheduled for the next day.

LEADER'S LAW: Creativity is a wonderful thing. I have a lot of admiration for people who can be creative and improvisational. They are often blessed with quick minds and they're often fun to be around, but they may or may not be good leaders. Creativity is just a quality that when added to the rest, is another arrow to be added to your quiver. If you don't seem to have that particular arrow in your own quiver, borrow one from someone else. They'll be flattered (usually).

ELEVEN

Circle the Wagons Boys, Here Comes an Indian

The sky is falling!
The sky is falling!

Chicken Little

Mark Twain once said, "Of all the problems that I ever had, most of them never happened." That may not be exactly right, but it's close. We spend a great deal of time worrying about things that never happen and very often waste a lot of time and effort to solve problems that don't exist. This is quite common among managers around the world. People tend to act on limited or early data. They begin a massive "Big Fix" when nothing is broken.

As some of you may remember, there was a time when all healthy young men who had no children and weren't in school were required to fulfill a military obligation. They could be drafted for two years of active duty followed by four years of active reserve or they could go down to a recruiting station and volunteer for six months active duty followed by five and one half years of active reserve. It was downright inconvenient and it was very difficult to get a job before the obligation had been met. One strategy was to take a break in college studies before graduation and join the reserve. Do the six months, come back, graduate, and you're ready to get on with your life. This is the route that I took. My career in the United States Coast Guard was almost totally without distinction other than the fact that for a time, I was the lowest ranking member of the national reserve program. This was because some Captain down in Miami couldn't take a joke, but that's a whole other story.

When I completed my active duty, I returned to college and was assigned to the Coast Guard Reserve unit in Athens, Georgia, as a clerk typist or apprentice yeoman or something like that. About the only requirement of the job was to hang out in the office until drill was over. Since I have never been one to suffer boredom gladly and there really wasn't anything to do, I began to look for things to occupy my hands until I could go home. The only things on my desk were an old Underwood typewriter and several different kinds of government stationary. What could I do with that?

My girlfriend, Becky, who shortly became my fiancée and eventually my wife, worked at a photography studio where most of the UGA pictures were taken and processed. Because of this, she was friendly with all of the university heavyweights from the president of the university on down. She was working full-time this quarter since her funds were running low.

One night the boredom got to me and I rolled a piece of that government stationary into the old Underwood, put in her work address at the top, and began "Greetings from the President of The United States." That's how all of the "notification of draft" letters began. "Dear Madam, You may be aware of the recent legislation which declares females to be eligible for the draft. You can be proud that you were selected to be one of the first inductees into the United States Army. There is no greater honor than being afforded the opportunity to serve one's country and I am sure that you will bear the banner with dignity and dedication."

It got a little more ridiculous as it went along. The last paragraph said, "You will report no later than 6:00 p.m. today to the recreation officer at Fort Alamo. He will give you your physical examination and you will be expected to follow his orders without question." The Alamo was the name that we had given to the place where seven other guys and I lived. It looked a bit like the Alamo (after the battle) and since the rent was only $40/month (total, not each) one couldn't expect a lavish layout. The letter was then closed as follows:

Love and affection,
The President
P.S. We may forego the physical if you'll cook a pot of chili.

The letter arrived at Becky's office two days later and she opened it and began to read. She made it through the first paragraph when she began to cry. This was not a sniffle. Loud sobbing could be heard, accompanied by many big tears. Her boss heard the noise and came to see what was wrong. Since she was too distraught to actually talk, she simply handed him the letter. He read the first paragraph and became incensed. "We'll see about that! They won't get away with this! We have important friends and this is NOT going to happen! President Aderhold is on his way in right now and we'll see what he has to say about it."

Can you guess what Dr. Aderhold did? You got it. He read the first paragraph and flew into action. He immediately called his secretary and instructed her to begin predated paperwork to get my girlfriend enrolled in school retroactively. That could be a felony. I don't know.

There happened to be another customer in the office at the time and he was apparently curious enough to pick up the letter and read it. He read it all and gave a great big laugh when he read the closing which I had signed as "The Prez." The panic was over, but when I heard about it, I was nervous for several days.

Was what I did illegal? It was government stationary, after all. The President's name was not used, but certainly his title. Why don't people get all the facts before running around frantically looking for a solution to a problem that never existed? If what I did was illegal, I'm sure that the statute of limitations has kicked in by now. The general reaction that took place in this story is not unusual, however. Every workplace of any size has at least one person working on a non-problem at all times, when another fact or two would save a lot of work and mental anguish.

 **LEADER'S LAW: Don't fix it until you find out it's really broken.**

Another good example of solving nonexistent problems is one that I heard from a colleague rather than witnessed myself. The story is so good, I feel that it must be passed on. Many of the old veterans in the consulting field got their start in mental health and it's a lot of fun to hear them sit around and tell war stories about the days at the hospital. One of my favorites seems to be appropriate to use here.

Mental disorder is not restricted to adults. Children are often victims and their treatments can be quite varied. Child psychologists, however, seem to agree that a child's schoolwork can be very revealing and helpful in determining a course of treatment.

One day in a meeting, a group of therapists were reviewing some artwork that was done by a little girl in their care. The picture that she had drawn was of a tree with a hole in the bottom of the trunk. This could be significant and each person was given time to present his interpretation of its meaning. One therapist, for example, said, "The hole obviously represents the womb. She has strong desires to return to the womb." Another offered, "The hole in the solid represents something that is missing in her life. She feels that her life will not be complete until the void is filled."

Their conversation went on for quite some time and eventually the little girl's teacher came into the room. She noticed the picture lying on the conference table and she smiled. "Isn't that sweet? We're studying the giant Redwoods and how they sometimes build roads right through them." I don't remember who I'm quoting here, but "Sometimes a cigar is just a cigar."

Very often, mistakes are made not because of inaccurate information, but because of not enough information. Find out everything that you can before taking action that might be disruptive and wasteful. It does not take a great deal of additional work to get ALL the facts together, and the savings in time and effort are usually great.

 **LEADER'S LAW: Collect as much reliable data as possible before making a decision or your actions may come back to bite you. (Also, never use stationery that you aren't authorized to use.)**

TWELVE

What Do You Want Me to Do?

I tried to treat them like me, and some of them weren't.

Coach Bill Russell on why he had difficulty with some of his players

Most of us have a large repertoire of skills that we draw from, depending upon the task at hand. When you are asked to vacuum the carpet, for example, you don't go for a hammer (unless you really are angry about being asked). We know from experience what has worked in the past and we choose the tool that will get the job done most expeditiously. Of course, if you've never seen a vacuum cleaner and have no idea that such a thing actually exists, we might be looking at a time-consuming project. Similar things happen to us every day.

One of the most negative things in business is the fact that people sometimes lose their jobs. I feel bad about it even if the person deserves it. I feel worse about it when it happens through no fault of the person. That's the way business is, however, and in the words of Don Corleone, "This is the life that we have chosen." That doesn't mean that we can't improve the situation. It's easy, really.

The first question in a person's mind as they begin any activity is, what do you want me to do? The question may never be spoken aloud and may never be answered in actual words. In those cases, we must answer our own question and that can be a risky proposition. When the boss says, "Welcome to the company and our little corporate family. Your office is down the hall. Get busy and increase sales!" he leaves quite a lot to interpretation. In a particular case that comes to mind, the boss should have added one comment to his little welcome speech. "Get busy and increase sales" should have been followed by "and do it exactly the way I would."

In this particular setting, as time passed, pressure mounted. The VP of sales' relationship with the CEO seemed to grow worse every day. He confided that he was putting out some feelers because the writing was on the wall. He expressed it as, "I'm dead meat."

When I asked the CEO about the VP's intuition, his response was, "He's right. He's doing the same old things that have been done for the last fifty years and haven't worked in twenty-five."

"Have you told him what you want him to do?" I asked.

He responded, "For what he's being paid, he damn sure ought to know what to do. I shouldn't have to tell him. I might as well do it myself."

The story ends badly, of course. The CEO never told him, the VP never successfully guessed, and life moved on. A man lost his job not because he didn't know how to do it, but because he didn't know exactly *what* doing the job looked like to his boss. Another good employee bit the dust and another valuable resource was squandered.

Situations such as this seem to happen fairly often although they don't get a great deal of discussion. I did no follow-up on this one, but there are many similar cases where the exact thing happened. The VP moved on to a similar job in a similar company and did great. Why?

Often, the boss doesn't know what he wants other than referring to the old bottom line. The employee is left with the task of deciding how to go about achieving the bottom-line goals. A wise person usually gathers as much information as he can before selecting a course of action. You have to admire a person who does that. A good case in point was Nub Garrett.

Years ago, I was doing some work for a textile company in South Carolina. The particular plant assignment took me to a very small rural town. There was no hotel. The company leased bedroom space in the back of a private home for employees who had to stay overnight. There was no movie theater and since cable hadn't reached that far yet, no TV. About the only thing to do at night was go down to the gas station and see who was filling up. Election time was always an exciting time. People discussed candidates, platforms, and their qualifications. Qualifications seemed to be fairly modest since one of the front running challengers for County Sheriff was a man named Boone Jackson, and everyone knew that he could neither read nor write.

One of the more interesting challengers was Nub Garrett. Nub dropped out of school after the ninth grade and went to work in the Carding Department at the local textile mill. Now carding machines can be tricky to operate. I have heard an estimate that a carding machine operator will lose a finger on an average of one about every four or five years. Nub worked on that job for thirty-five years. You can do the math. The first four or five finger deletions didn't affect his life all that much (other than people giving him his well-earned nickname), but now that he was down to three fingers he thought it might be time to seek a new line of work. He decided to run for office. Tax assessor and tax collector were out because everybody hated taxes and anybody who had anything to do with them. Coroner seemed to have potential since he would be dealing with dead people for the most part and they rarely complained about anything. It was a fun race, but we won't go into that right now.

Boone won the sheriff position even though he was in jail on Election Day. The incumbent sheriff thought that this would certainly give him an edge, but Boone won anyway. Nub also won his race for coroner. People seemed to be impressed with his pre-election preparation and his comments about how he would go about discharging the duties of the job.

Three weeks into the new term, Nub got a call in the middle of the night. It was Boone. Some coon hunters had discovered an unidentified dead body in the woods. Apparently Nub was not the only one to get the call. When he arrived, there were about twenty people milling around the scene. No one had any idea who the unfortunate late person was. He was lying on his face and since he had obviously been there for quite some time, no one would touch him to turn him over. Nub sprang into action. He turned the body over and determined that he had never seen him before. He went through the man's pockets only to find that there was no identification there. He then called a conference with Boone. "My suggestion is this," Nub said. "There's twenty people here who wuz born and raised right here in the county. Let's get 'em to file by. Surely somebody'll know who he is." So they did it and the results were discouraging. Nobody knew who this guy was. Then Nub showed his preparation. All of his reading was about to pay off. He told Boone, "They ain't but one thing left that I know to do. We'll just box this feller up and send him down to Columbia." Columbia, of course, is where the state pathology lab is located.

Boone was shocked and appalled. He said, "I ain't gonna tell anybody that. It's the dumbest idea that I ever heard, Nub. You'll be the laughin' stock of the whole county."

"Why?" asked Nub.

"You must not be thinkin' Nub. We wuz all born and raised right here in this area. If none of us know him, you know dang well ain't nobody down in Columbia gonna know him."

Nub found out what to do and how to get it done. Boone had no idea that bodies could be identified by forensic experts.

 **LEADER'S LAW: As a leader, you don't have to know everything if you're wise enough to use the talents of those around you.**

Many manufacturing facilities in the South are owned by larger corporations which are often headquartered in the North. When an executive from the home office has scheduled a visit to the plant, the local management wants to have the place looking clean and neat. The plant manager's name was Chick and he gave the order, "Clean it up boys, company's coming." They worked very hard and they were all proud of their results. However, when Chick made his rounds, he was furious. "When I say 'Clean it up,' I mean clean it up!"

They went back to work on it and the next morning Chick made another round. If anything, he was madder after this inspection than the first. "It's still a mess," he shouted. "Clean it up by this afternoon or I swear I'll fire the whole bunch of you."

A supervisor was heard to say, "Man, I'd eat grits off that floor. What does he want?" One of my colleagues happened to be in there that day and realized that this situation was going from bad to worse. As he went through the plant with Chick, and after a fair amount of time was spent listening to him vent, he asked, "What is it that you don't like, Chick? I gotta admit that it looks good to me." With that, Chick began to itemize the things that needed to be done. When he finished, my colleague said, "I'll bet you $10 they will have all those problems corrected by lunch." Chick took the bet. My friend then took his list of transgressions and passed it off to a supervisor who smiled and said, "So that's what he wants."

After lunch they made another plant tour and guess what. It was perfect. Chick couldn't believe it. "How did they do that?" The answer, of course, was, "I told them what you wanted." Chick thought for a minute and then he said, "That's cheating. I ain't about to pay off that bet."

That example is a bit extreme, sure, but it is not unusual. We do it all the time. Do you have children? Would you like to have them do a better job of cleaning their rooms? How do you ask them to do it? A very high percentage of the time, we say something like, "This room looks like an explosion at the Salvation Army! Clean it up right now!" What are the odds that you will be pleased with the results? Probably low. The child didn't realize that you are concerned about the month-old pizza under the mattress or the mud on the carpet.

 **LEADER'S LAW: If you want to be an effective leader, make yourself easy to follow. Go ahead and provide the answer to that often unspoken question, what do you want me to do?**

THIRTEEN

How Am I Doing?

The very first step toward success
in any occupation
is to become interested in it.

Sir William Osler

The second most important question that a person asks is, "How am I doing?" We need to know if we're moving in the right direction or getting farther and farther away from our goal or destination. Without this information, progress may seem hopeless. It isn't, of course. It's just frustratingly slow.

Let's dip into science just a little bit and see if we can avoid a lot of frustration. The scientific definition of feedback is *"information on past performance that helps you improve your performance."* The definition is cleverly worded in that the information doesn't count unless it helps.

Several years ago, I was taking a class in scuba diving at the local YMCA. About twenty students were in the class and one night the instructor had us doing laps in the pool by utilizing the flutter kick. After about fifteen minutes, the instructor announced, "About half of you are doing it wrong, but let's go on to something else." When we got out of the pool, a lady asked me, "Which half were you in?" To this day, I still don't know if I am a good flutter kicker. The good news is that I have always managed to get back to the boat and that, after all, is probably the most important part.

In most cases, when we don't get the information we need, we tend to develop our own measures. A novel was published several years ago with a main character, a high-rolling Texan by the name of Cash McCall. Someone asked him, "Why do you keep wheeling and dealing? You have more money than you can ever spend."

"The money ain't important for what it will buy," McCall answered. "It's just a way to keep score."

I suppose that money could be a form of feedback. The point is that we usually need information about how we're doing somewhere between the beginning and the end. For example, when my son was small and playing baseball in a league managed by the YMCA, they came up with an interesting concept. They announced at the beginning of the season that the object of playing was to have fun and to develop the skills to become proficient in the game. Therefore, no scorekeeping would be allowed during the coming season. All players would all be winners simply for participating. Can you guess what happened? The first few games were so frustrating that the parents started keeping score. Between every inning, the kids would come to the fence in front of the seating section and ask, "What's the score?" Parents would dutifully whisper a word of encouragement along with the current number of runs for each team. I never saw a kid get depressed after losing a game by twenty runs or so, but I did see a great deal of frustration and arguing develop from not knowing. It was a concept that just didn't work.

We *need* to know how we're doing. If you are to be an effective leader, you must not only be prepared to provide this information, you must provide it regularly! Is a person going in the right direction and making progress or moving away from the direct path and wasting a great deal of time with false starts and dead ends?

How about doing a little field test here? You need at least four or five people to do it, but the more, the merrier. When your kids have a few friends over would be a good time to try this test, although it works just as well with adults. Ask three people to leave the room. Hide a dollar bill in a place where it will be difficult to find. Bring in the first participant and explain that there is a dollar bill hidden in this room and if they can find it, they can keep it. Give them a limit of five minutes to find it. Everyone else must remain silent, and they cannot help the seeker in any way. Keep the time even though the person, in all probability, will not find the dollar. Be ready to duck. It's a small amount of money but they may get frustrated, then angry.

Now we will give them some help. When we bring in the second participant, we will tell him when he is going in the wrong direction by having those in the room say "cold" whenever he or she moves in a direction that is away from the dollar. When they move in the direction of the dollar, there should be silence. It's a small twist on the game most of us have played as children. Receiving only the clues of cold, the second person may find it before the five minutes are up. A lot depends upon how well the dollar is hidden. They will certainly come closer than participant number one.

Now we will give participant number three some *good* feedback. You might want to save this spot for your own kid thereby keeping the dollar in the family. We will say "cold" when he or she moves away from the dollar and we will say "warm," "warmer," or "hot" when the movement is in the correct direction. In this case, no matter how well the dollar is hidden, the third participant who received the best feedback will find the money in well under five minutes. This little experiment is not dissimilar to situations that we encounter on a daily basis. Most failures are a result of too little information during the process or, in other terms, a *feedback deficiency.*

It's really quite amazing what a person can accomplish when they have adequate feedback. We have much more control of our own bodies than was initially thought. We just need more information in order to make this control work for us. In the early '70s, I predicted that by the end of the millennium we would not need nearly as many doctors. This was because biofeedback (information on how our bodies are working at the moment) was developing at an astonishing rate. People were actually eliminating discomfort by adjusting the output of various organs in their own bodies.

If your daughter or son is engaged to a doctor, do not be alarmed. My prediction didn't work out. We still need doctors and I suspect that we always will. I had a chance to try biofeedback myself, though, and found it to be very interesting. I was part of the instruction team at a workshop being held in Atlanta. While I was in front of the group, I began to have some very strange symptoms. It occurred to me that I might be having a stroke. I left the workshop and went to a hospital where I expressed my concern. They flew into action and in just a very short time had connected me to several machines that I had never seen before. Note: Just so that you won't become overly upset as I describe this drama as it played out, I break in to tell you that I was not having a stroke or anything life threatening. It was an allergy to a particular brand of brass polish that was commonly used in the hotel. I lived.

It didn't take them long to pronounce me a natural wonder of good health. That didn't, however, mean that I was cleared as being fit to return to work. They insisted that I stay until the results of the blood work-up were in. Their instructions were, "Just lay here on the table. It shouldn't take much more than an hour."

MUCH MORE THAN AN HOUR? There was nothing to read. There were no windows. The door was closed. Since I was still connected to the machines, I couldn't get up and walk around. How long would it be before I started screaming? Then I noticed a TV monitor located high on a wall in the corner of the room. It was on, but no good program was showing at the time and there was no remote control in sight. The only thing that was on the screen was a little squiggly line that we all know from the many medical TV shows that we watch. It means that the patient's heart is beating. When the line becomes flat, it means that a dedicated doctor is going to come in and shock us (hopefully in time for resuscitation). At the bottom of the screen was a number. It was 66. What was that? Pulse rate? My next thought was, I wonder if I can speed that up? If I could increase my pulse rate, it would have to be done without moving. I was still connected to the machines, after all. My next question to myself was, What is the best way to do it, since I can't exercise?

How about fright? Let's think about that one. It might work. What scares me more than anything else? That's easy—snakes. Since I used to step on a rattlesnake about every other day, I should be able to resurrect a vivid memory of that. When I did it, I looked up to see that my pulse rate had increased to 68. This was encouraging. If you saw the miniseries *Lonesome Dove,* you may recall that the first episode ended with a still photograph of a water moccasin with its fangs sunken in a child's cheek. That image caused me to sleep fitfully for a night or two and it had a similar effect on my pulse rate when I simply recalled the scene. The number rose to 70.

Could I make it go the other way? Could I slow my pulse rate down? Yes, I could, by simply following the opposite strategy. My Pa was never one to place a high value on getting ahead of schedule. If we had a good morning, we would often go to the creek, swim, and nap on the creek bank. This was the most peaceful time that I could remember. Guess what? As I thought about those lazy days, my pulse rate went down to as low as 64. I spent the rest of my hospital stay playing with my pulse. (There's no shame in this if you don't get caught.) I eventually reached a point where I could increase or decrease the rate without the use of mind pictures. I include this example to make a point, of course. You will probably never have a similar opportunity, I hope, but many situations arise in which a working knowledge of self-feedback, also known as *biofeedback,* can serve you well.

An example of performance feedback (not biofeedback), which occurred in a plant, proved to be very moving. A supervisor, who had made great strides in helping to raise the productivity of his department, decided that he had reached the point where a bit of fine-tuning was in order. He identified his lowest performer and began a feedback process for her. He spent five minutes with her two to three times each day. He also met with her at the end of every shift to review and summarize her performance. Her efficiency increased every day until she was among the top performers in the department. Here is the part that moved me.

One day, the same supervisor was working in his office when another long-term poor performer knocked on his open door. She self-consciously approached his desk and asked, "Whatever you're doing for Joyce, could you do it for me too?"

It is important to note that these operators were not being paid by the piece or so-called incentive pay. Low performers were paid the same hourly wage as the top performers. In effect, this worker was saying, "I want to be good at my job. Please help me do that."

 **LEADER'S LAW: Most people want to succeed at whatever they do. A good leader will show employees how to succeed.**

FOURTEEN

Want Some More?
Give Some Away

Money is like manure.
It doesn't do any good unless you
spread it around.

Dolly Levi

Not many people get rich through saving their money if saving is all they ever do. Most people get rich by one of two ways: 1) their rich and generous father dies, or 2) they save and invest. They make their savings grow. Leadership is very much like that. If we want more money, we have to be willing to give some away.

Years ago, I was asked to write an article for a trade magazine addressing the question of what is the optimal number of employees that one person can effectively manage. That is a great deal like the old question, "How much wood could a woodchuck chuck if a woodchuck could chuck wood?" The answer, of course, is that it depends almost entirely upon the individual woodchuck. Some are better at chucking wood than others. The same is true of managers and leaders. Some micromanage and have to be involved in every aspect of a process, while others delegate responsibility and nurture leadership skills in those who want to progress. People *can* lead and follow at the same time.

As mentioned in a previous chapter, my first job after college was in the textile industry and I did nothing else for the next ten years. Things were pretty good in those days. There was no foreign competition to speak of and most companies were content to keep their own manufacturing interests in the USA. Business was good. The most significant problem facing businesses at that time was one of employee turnover. All companies were fairly similar in terms of working conditions, pay, required skills, benefits, and so on. Another similarity was that all companies needed workers. It was not unusual for some people to work for ten or more different employers during the course of one year and never miss a day of work. Executives spent many hours discussing the problem and not reaching any conclusions. The problem, of course, was simple. It was the solution that was complex, even though we would much rather have it the other way around. The problem was that people just didn't like their jobs and they kept moving around in an effort to find a better situation.

In the textile operation where I worked, the most difficult position to keep filled was that of doffer. A yarn doffer's job was to remove full bobbins from spinning machines and replace them with empty bobbins so that we could wind more yarn. The problem solvers saw this as a very good job. It was easy (no heavy lifting), indoors, and regular. So why did they have to stop machines and lose production because there was often no one on the job to remove the full bobbins? Does doffing sound like an exciting job to you? Well, it wasn't. It was downright boring!

I remember attending morning production meetings. Every day, the plant manager would glare at the poor department manager of the Spinning Department and ask, "Why didn't you make production?" The department manager would reply, "I ain't got no doffers." Then the plant manager would say, "Oh." That was it. What could anybody do?"

This was an industry-wide problem. One of the professional organizations came up with an idea, or maybe they got it from a PR firm. It was The National Doffer Competition. It was like the Super Bowl of doffing. The big competition was held once each year and a new champion was crowned. The new champion was written up in all the trade magazines and his picture was often prominently displayed in living color on the cover. This guy must have felt great (at least during this short stint of fame). Unfortunately, the rest of the doffers remained bored.

After leaving the textile industry and spending some time in the consulting business, I was called upon to visit a textile plant in Georgia. In my first meeting with the plant manager there, I naturally wanted to sound knowledgeable, so I asked, "How are you managing the doffer problem?"

He replied with a very blank, "Huh?"

"The doffer problem. How do you handle the absenteeism and turnover problem, especially with doffers?" I asked again. I was almost floored by his next statement.

"Why, I haven't lost a doffer in years." It was my turn to look blank. "It used to be a problem," he continued, "but I got tired of dealing with it every day. I called them all together and passed the problem on to them. They make most of the decisions that affect their jobs. They discuss what needs to be done, they decide if overtime is needed, and they determine who should be called upon if it is. If Saturday work is required, they decide how much and who. If they need something, they let me know."

The technology of automatic doffing equipment has in recent years eliminated the problem of *bored* doffers by eliminating the need for doffers, but the principal of this story still holds true. An effective leader does not have to solve every problem himself.

Another example involved a high-end, multilocation furniture manufacturer. They produced heirloom quality furniture. The only thing wrong with that furniture is that when you die, all the kids argue about who gets it. They all say, "Mama always said that she wanted me to have that table." Hard feelings over such can linger for years.

The workers were not paid on a production rate for fear that quality might suffer. Their compensation was based on a flat hourly rate. One operation was headed by a very personable fellow named Whiz. The productivity of his department had been lagging behind for as long as anyone could remember and poor Whiz heard about it quite often. He had tried everything he knew to do. Productivity just never got any better. I helped him formulate a plan that I felt might get things moving in the right direction. As he went about carrying out some of my preliminary suggestions before getting started, one of his workers came up to him and asked, "What's going on Whiz?"

Whiz scratched his chin for a minute and then said, "I'll tell you what's going on. I get yelled at every day for low production and I'm getting tired of it. We just have to do better."

The worker smiled and said, "Hell, that ain't no problem. How many do you need?"

This was not the response that Whiz was expecting, but he gathered his wits and answered, "We're getting around thirty drawers built per hour right now and we need thirty-eight per hour."

The worker then said, "We can do better than that."

"No," Whiz said, "we don't want a big number. We want the *right* number."

The worker went back to the line and called an impromptu meeting. At the end of the discussion, they all nodded their heads and went back to work. From that point on, they produced thirty-eight drawers per hour or very close to it. How did they do it? It seems simple. The worker at the end of the line who removed the finished product and passed it on to the next operation kept count. Every hour he posted the number produced during the previous hour so that everyone on the line could see it. With that information available for them to see, they adjusted their pace to comply with the engineered standards and still maintained their required quality. They generated their own feedback and in the process they provided answers to two of the questions that we have discussed in previous chapters: 1) What do you want me to do? and 2) How am I doing? I liked the fact that they decided what they needed and provided it for themselves. Not every problem has to have a complex answer. Sometimes the answer can be quite simple and you need do nothing to solve it other than ask.

There is a gentleman with whom I worked for many years who has what he calls "The Leisurely Theorem of Management." He's a bright guy and it's always worth the time to sit down and hear some of the things that he has been thinking about. Basically, he says that a truly good leader will not have to do a great deal of leading. The great leader will take the time to cultivate leadership skills within his followers. Then he needs only to stop by the office about once a week to tell everyone that they're doing a good job and thank them for doing so. If he takes his time and does this correctly, he will still have plenty of time to get in eighteen holes of golf before going back home.

Does this sound good to you? In theory, it sounds great. I have noticed, however, that this guy comes to the office on most days. It would seem to be something to strive for as long as we realize that we are unlikely to reach that level of competence in our leadership. He does fall into a category of leaders that I call macromanagers. The majority of people who worked for him were allowed to go about doing things their own way and at their own speed. The level of freedom was uncommon. It was the best thing about the job.

If you can get people in a work group to demonstrate their approval of each other's performance, you can have a good thing going. Some of you may be familiar with an experiment that was undertaken by the San Diego Chargers football club. They contracted with a psychologist to give up his practice for a year and devote his full time to the team. At the end of the year, he was to write a report of his findings. Presumably, this would help the team win more football games the next year. I was eager to read the report.

Actually, he came up with only two interesting things. The first and most mildly interesting of the two was his claim that he could look at a player's locker and, from the locker's condition, accurately determine the position that the occupant played. His determination was based upon the degree of messiness. Would you like to guess before I give you the answer? Did you guess that the neatness award goes to the quarterback? Sorry, you're wrong. That is the majority answer, however, so don't beat yourself up.

The correct answer is that the offensive linemen have the neatest lockers. They tend to be very focused and organized. They always have an assignment to carry out and there is very little room for improvisation; therefore, neat locker. The messy locker award goes to linebackers, with defensive backs coming in at a close second. Now for the most important question of all: WHO CARES? I certainly don't and I don't think anyone with the Chargers cared either, even though it did provide a tidbit of trivia. Let's move on to the next major discovery.

Football players, like most everyone else, have priorities. Approval of their performance is important to them, but the degree of importance varies depending upon from whom the approval originates. Whose approval do you think is the most powerful to the player? The coach? Nope. He's in second place. The fans? Nope again. They're third. Sportswriters? *Way no!* They're like fourth. So, what is the most important source of approval for a player in the National Football League? The answer is: approval from teammates. That bit of information may not help them win football games, but I thought that it was very interesting and it has helped me in working with people in almost any industry or occupation. We look to our peers for approval. Usually, peers are happy to provide it if they see it as being important or meaningful.

 **LEADER'S LAW: A manager's to-do list may be quite long, but it should always include reward leadership.**

FIFTEEN

I Think That Went Rather Well, Don't You?

Be careful which behaviors you reinforce, because you will surely get more of them

Aubrey C. Daniels

Hopefully, you now have gained better knowledge and ability for influencing the behavior of others. The more you use this knowledge and ability, the more influence you will have. As is the case of any skill that we attempt to improve, it takes some practice and fine-tuning. Now comes the scary part.

The ability to influence the behavior of others can be used as a definition of the word power. Influence is *power* and, as such, should be used responsibly. If you have the ability to strengthen the behaviors of other people, this is a power that should not be taken lightly. When you strengthen behaviors, you are causing them to happen more often.

Ole' Junior, my snake-hunting yard dog, risked his life daily for a pat on the head. No one meant for that to happen, but it did. Most of our behaviors are shaped and strengthened in much the same way: that is to say, by accident.

When we plan our approach to changing behavior, it should be noted that there are three possible outcomes. The first is that our strategy worked. That, of course, is what we intended. The second is that it didn't work. This should not cause you a great deal of despair. Simply rethink it and start again. The third possible outcome, if it happens, can result in a bit more of a problem. What if it works TOO well? Once a behavior is established and strengthened, it is sometimes difficult to change.

A good case in point is the reward programs that have been created by the airlines. They worked too well. They were intended to create customer loyalty. Once the customer started accumulating points, he or she was inclined to choose the airline that would add points and result in a free ticket, a free upgrade, improved boarding priority, or some other benefit. Travelers began to save their points and make plans. Some saved their points and made plans to make plans later. Those were a problem. If everyone decided to use their point awards on the same day, it would prove disastrous to the airline.

I have a friend who saved over a million points in his frequent-flyer account. The cost of a first-class, round-trip ticket to most anywhere cost only around 50,000 points at the time. From my home location, I could upgrade to first class and the result was that the points that were added to my account exceeded the cost of the upgrade. Obviously, this became a dangerous situation for the airlines.

Every year for the last few years, the airlines have notified their regular customers that the frequent-flyer program is being modified to "better serve you." Even the best spin master is going to have a difficult time explaining how the customer will be better served by having his program benefits cut.

The frequent-flyer program was simply too good. If the customer views the situation objectively, it's easy to understand why the changes were necessary. Customers, however, are not really big on objectivity and a large number of them got angry. For awhile, it was a major topic being discussed at boarding gates and waiting areas in airports across the country. Slipping these kinds of changes past a person who travels for a living is about as likely as slipping the sunrise past a rooster. It can't be done. The bottom line is that travelers are now paying more attention to the things that they should have been paying attention to all along. Schedules and ticket prices have now been restored to their proper place at the top of the customer priority list. The program did what the airlines wanted it to do, but it worked too well.

 **LEADER'S LAW: When you're making a plan to change behavior, you'd better consider what will happen if your plan works too well.**

As a result of congressional testimony, wrestling has been reclassified as an entertainment and not a sport. Rather than a physical contest between two people, it is a small pageant involving the wrestlers and the referee. Take a look at it on TV the next time you're channel surfing through video land. Look at the behavior of the fans. You'll see that their behavior (for that particular sport) is approximately the same as it has always been. People get emotional. The combatants (i.e. actors, tumblers, and exhibitionists) incite emotion in the audience. The more they do this, the more in demand they become.

At one point, I lived next door to a wrestler. He seemed to be a pretty good guy, but I never got to know him that well since he worked at night and I worked days.

Our wives were friends though, and we were usually invited over on those occasions when they had company or a party. Their friends were mostly wrestlers and I noticed that when we got together, it was a fairly even mix of villains and heroes. They were all nice people. The villains were not villainous and the heroes were not heroic. They were just nice people who enjoyed the company of others and because they could elicit an emotional response from their audience, they made a comfortable living.

In my hometown, we had wrestling every week at the National Guard Armory. One of the wrestlers (a disgusting bad guy) always came to town early in the day and sat around with my dad until time to go to the armory. I don't know how that relationship began, but there it was. For this guy, job security came with being hated; therefore he loved the people who hated him. One of those people, Luther Knuckles, had been wounded in World War II and walked with the use of a cane. Every week, Luther became so upset that he left his ringside seat, waved his cane in the air, and charged the ring. The wrestlers played to him. He was as much fun to watch as the show.

One night, however, their act worked too well. The Vickers brothers, Lard and Spud, were in attendance and taking bets as they always did. A lot of gambling went on regarding the outcome of these matches. (How weird is that?) Generally, the Vickers always bet on the hero because he always won. Consequently, this was usually a pretty profitable night for them.

The loser, on this particular night, was the mysterious Masked Marvel. No one knew who he was, but he had pledged to remove his mask if he lost. He lost the first match, of course, but then he refused to remove his mask. Lard and Spud had made a big investment in the hero that night and when the Masked Marvel made a comeback in the next match and whipped the hero, it was more than they could stand. They jumped into the ring and proceeded to beat the living dickens out of the Masked Marvel. The hero made a sprint to the dressing room and locked the door behind him. The referee, to his credit, tried to help, only to be pitched over the top rope by Spud.

I had never really thought about it, but those masks are very difficult to remove. The Masked Wonder was laced into that thing with a rawhide strip. Lard decided to cut the mask off, but when he took his knife out of his pocket, everyone thought that he was going to cut the Marvel's throat and the police started going for their guns. He wisely decided to put his knife away and unlace the mask by hand. The police were uncomfortable with the idea of confronting either Lard *or* Spud. Lard and Spud proceeded to take that discomfort to a whole new level.

There were only three policemen at the ring and one of them excused himself due to a prior commitment to direct traffic at the close of a revival meeting at Morningside Drive Baptist Church. That left only two, but they gamely began to carefully climb into the ring. Spud had appropriated a metal folding chair and was beating the police away from the ring while Lard gave his undivided attention to getting that darn mask off of the Marvel. When they finally got the mask off, the Marvel turned out to be a guy who had wrestled earlier in the evening. The Vickers boys were so disgusted and deflated that they allowed themselves to be taken off to jail without any resistance. I don't think they were actually locked up. They called off the matches for the next week because the wrestlers were afraid to come back and I can't blame them. It even scared Luther. The wrestlers' job was to incite the crowd. That night they did their job too well.

Most mistakes are made by people who have the best

of intentions. Their hearts are pure and their motives are most honorable. They just didn't quite get their plan right and in some cases they never thought that it would work to the point of excess. There is an old saying about good intentions paving the way to hell.

I worked with a company a couple of years ago that fell into that kind of situation. They had some concerns regarding their safety incentive program and asked that I give it a look. Their intentions were admirable. They realized that accidents are expensive and a great deal of money could be saved if they could cause a significant decrease in their incident rate. They decided that a nice thing to do would be to share the savings with their employees in the form of a check paid directly to every individual who did not have an accident during the previous year. This check was paid at Christmas time. Even though it was called a safety bonus, it felt like a Christmas bonus. Within a very short time, everyone looked forward to it as a given and counted on that extra money to help with the expenses of the season.

The amount of the check was significant. I was shocked. We're talking serious money here. To have an accident was a calamity not only because of the injury to the person, but because of the loss of money at a time when they needed it (or wanted it) most. Can you guess what happened?

Hopefully, you know enough about human behavior at this point to predict the outcome if you think about the situation in terms of why people do the things that they do. What was the money contingent upon? Did it make people work more carefully? This is a bit tricky, so I'll move right along.

The bonus was calculated on the basis of accidents REPORTED. The employee would lose the bonus only if he or she reported the accident. Employees actually continued to have accidents. We just don't know how many accidents they had because they were reported only when it was absolutely necessary. People would actually slip out and go to a walk-in clinic to get sewn up and then pay for it out of their own pockets to avoid reporting the mishap. Then they returned to work before the end of the shift and clocked out on time. Supervisors were included in this bonus program, so slipping out may not have been as difficult as one might imagine. Reporting an accident to management was no fun.

The bad news is that the program did not do what was intended. The worst news is that once something like that is established and employees are looking forward to the payoff, it is extremely difficult to get out of it. How can you take it away and still avoid serious morale problems? It's a dangerous act to take something away from a person who considers it an entitlement. He or she likes it just the way it is and they don't want anyone messing with it.

At least if you must take something away, the change is easier and less traumatic if you give something new to replace it. The only thing out of place in this instance is that the bonus supported the wrong behaviors. On paper, the bonus plan was a roaring success. In real life, it was not. The employees were doing what they were doing (putting themselves and others in more danger by not reporting accidents and the causes of those accidents) for an excellent reason. They were getting paid for it. The task in such a situation then becomes identifying the things that we *really* want people to do and then making sure that they get something for it. If a company has made one of these incentive flaws, making the change will never be a fun experience.

 **LEADERSHIP LESSON: Consider all of the possible behaviors that could be encouraged if you are only recognizing the result. Then adjust incentive plans accordingly**

SIXTEEN

What's In It for Me?

When I walk down the street,
I want people to say
"There goes Roy Hobbs,
the best *there ever was*."

Roy Hobbs, *The Natural*

We have addressed the first two questions: 1) What do you want me to do? and 2) How am I doing? To complete the cycle we need to take a look at another question: What's in it for me? This is the question that closes the deal. If you can't supply a good answer for this one, the first two have been a waste of your time. To make matters more difficult, most people haven't a clue as to what others want. We think that we know, but we're often way off.

The quote at the top of the page comes from the baseball movie *The Natural*. Just about everybody in the civilized world (at least all of us baseball fans) has seen in. I've watched it several times. It must be showing somewhere on some television channel at any given time during the day, and whenever I land on it, I can't seem to leave it. Roy Hobbs, the central character in the movie, wanted above all else to be the best player of the game. So what's so unusual about that? Everybody would like to be the best there ever was at something. I know that I would. The question then becomes, How much are you willing to pay to achieve your dreams? What is a reasonable price? Would the risk of death be reasonable? How about certain death? While these prices may be reasonable to some, they are way too high for most of us. Maybe that is why there is only one best in most endeavors.

I read an article a few years ago that examined the results of a survey that had been given to Olympic athletes. Several athletes had been caught using performance enhancing drugs even though the drug had been identified as being potentially dangerous to the consumer. Some very pointed questions were asked and the athletes were very forthcoming with their answers.

Several interesting points came from this survey. While the athletes realized the risks, they never believed for a second that they would personally suffer any physical harm from taking the drugs. They never believed that they would have to pay that price. The real risk, in their minds, was the possibility of being caught and disqualified from Olympic competition.

Perhaps most shocking was their response to a hypothetical question: If a drug were available that would guarantee a gold medal performance in your event followed by certain death within one year, would you take that drug? Over 60 percent answered yes! That gave me a chill, so let's move on to some activities that don't require this type (perhaps twisted) of commitment.

Almost every transaction will go through a certain process whether that transaction is in the realm of work or leisure. For example, my knees are a total wreck and I can't do yard work as I once could. The solution to my problem seemed to be to contact a young person blessed with an abundance of energy. I knew of a college student in the neighborhood who needed some part- time work so I gave him a call and asked him if he'd do the work before my neighbors started to leave nasty notes in my mailbox. As I outlined the tasks that needed to be done, his response was a solemn nod. Then he asked, "What's in it for me?" The answer was forty dollars.

He shook his head, chewed his lower lip, and gener-ally conveyed his feelings that this was a tough decision. Then he took my hand and shook it before I had time to rethink my offer. I saw very little of him after that. In the weeks that followed, he cut the grass at Mach I speed and was usually out of sight before the sound of his weed whacker had died away. He was so fast that I began to have second thoughts about our deal. Considering the time and effort that he took, twenty dollars should have been plenty. However, in my mind, you can no more renege on an agreement than you can unshoot a gun. To this day, I continue to pay him forty dollars. Today, I sel-dom see him at all, nor do any of his customers. He has hired other people to drive his big trucks and use his industrial-sized lawnmowers, weed eaters, and leaf blow-ers. He dropped out of college, due to his growing and successful business, so the world will have to survive with one less lawyer. (Wait a minute; maybe that's the real upside of this story.)

The point is that all of us are engaged in some type of give-and-take transaction every day, with the pivotal outcome determined by what's in it for the parties involved. Even animals are involved in these types of transactions. My dog Rufus, for example, does not seem to be the least bit motivated by approval. He's an English bulldog and the book on this breed says that his take on approval is somewhat atypical. He does, however, respond very well to treats. The result of this, when we first got

Rufus, was a very fat dog that was eager to respond to simple commands. However, when we tried to do something about the weight situation, we discovered that apparently low fat, low calorie doggie treats don't taste any better than low fat, low calorie people treats. Rufus soon decided that the payoff was not worth the effort and subsequently he became less enthusiastic about following commands. If he could only eat unlimited quantities of cheese, I'm pretty sure that I could teach him to play the banjo or maybe even to juggle.

Several things must be considered when making decisions about motivating people (and probably animals).

1) It's sometimes difficult to know what every person likes. We know what *we* like, so typically we suspect that everyone likes the same things that we like. All too often, they do not. To complicate things further, we try to make those odd people enjoy the things that they would surely like if we only presented those things in the right way. For example, I don't like chocolate and I never have liked chocolate. People just can't believe this astounding fact. They prepare it in different ways: cakes, cookies, fudge, brownies. Some have even tried to catch me secretly eating chocolate. For a lifetime, I've heard the breathless question, "How can you not like chocolate?" Therefore, to save myself the agony, whenever a host puts a chocolate dessert in front of me, I say, "This looks really great, but I'm allergic to all forms of chocolate. A single bite is enough to put me in a coma." Believe it or not, even this excuse doesn't work at times. PLEASE NOTE: The examples discussed so far in this chapter relate to tangible things that people can touch, spend, or taste. While many people proclaim that intangible

things are better for motivating others, those intangibles also have pitfalls. You have probably read articles, books, and papers that proclaim the power of "being in on things." Supposedly, people will go to great lengths when the end result of the transaction is that they will be in on things. This may be true of some people, but it isn't true of everyone. Many people will go to great lengths to avoid being in on things.

2) Don't get yourself into an awkward position by agreeing to provide (contingently, of course) something that can't or shouldn't be delivered. Even though your 10-year-old did a terrific job of washing the car, you might not want to reward him with a cold beer and the car keys. In a work setting, you can promise a cash bonus, a raise in pay, or a promotion *only* if you can deliver same. The following conversation actually took place between me and a department manager of a medium-sized manufacturing plant.

Manager: I'm in trouble.

Me: Why?

Manager: I promised my people a cash bonus if they reached production goals.

Me: And?

Manager: They reached the goals.

Me: Is that bad?

Manager: Yes, because I don't have the authority to give cash bonuses.

Me: Why did you make the promise if you knew that you couldn't deliver?

Manager: I didn't think they would ever reach the goals.

Me: I would like from you a signed memo stating that I had nothing whatsoever to do with this and that I had absolutely no advance knowledge of this plan.

As with most things that we attempt to do, there are virtually unlimited ways to mess up. Let's save some time here and go over a few steps we can take to make our efforts to motivate people as effective as possible.

First and foremost: Talk to people. Ask them what they like and what they want. They will tell you. The problem is that they will often tell you what they think you want to hear, especially if you hold a position of authority over them. Watch out.

Secondly, observe people as they go about their day. When they have a choice of work-related things to do, which do they select?

In his book *Praise for Profit,* Jerry Pounds discusses in detail how the trivialization of a person's work effort can demotivate that person very quickly, so I have. This inspired me to created an example of how this trivialization might occur.

Boss: Due to your hard work for the last three months, we have realized record profits for the quarter. In recognition, I would like to present you with this baseball cap. As you can see, it's a real beauty. It has the company logo on the front and one of these adjustable things in the back, so you can tighten it up. Thanks, Jim Bob!

Jim Bob: Hogwash! (Jim Bob is a religious man who never used harsh language.)

Boss: That ungrateful ingrate.

According to some books, Jim Bob should have felt very good about his performance and rededicated his efforts to do even better from now on. In real life, Jim Bob would have wanted to tell the boss off in words that he hadn't used since he got religion. Jim Bob was turned off, as most of us would have been. This is trivialization of a work effort (and the performer's intelligence).

Several years ago, my boss got a call from one of my high school friends. We hadn't seen each other since graduation, and it was pure coincidence that he contacted my employer. He stated his problem basically as, "I own two retail carpet outlet stores and I employ 12 people. They are okay workers, but they have no sense of urgency. I want them to work like I do. I want them to work like they own a piece of the company. How do I get that kind of commitment from them?

My boss's profound answer was, "Give them a piece of the company."

My friend's first thought (as he related to me later) was, "I hope he isn't going to bill me for that piece of advice." As time passed, however, he began to think about what my boss had said. He designed an employee ownership plan. In a very short time, his employees were working like they owned a piece of the company? Know why? Because they did.

 **LEADERSHIP LESSON: Find out how people want to be rewarded, and if at all possible, arrange a way for them to earn it.**

SEVENTEEN

Complete the Puzzle:
See the Big Picture

If fear is cultivated, it will become stronger.
If faith is cultivated it will achieve mastery.

John Paul Jones

Okay. You pretty much have all the basics now. Let's direct our attention to putting it all together. As stated earlier, when it comes to leadership we should try to answer three questions: What do you want me to do? How am I doing? What's in it for me? I'm going to give you some rather specific examples, but the specifics will not, in all probability, apply to you and your particular situation. The examples are intended to show how some people took the concepts that I have discussed and applied their own real-life variables.

I had a client a few years ago who was located in a small town in Missouri. The company was a small, individually owned manufacturing operation, and they had done a lot of things well over the years. The engineering manager was a young man who was very excited about improving his leadership skills using the ideas that I have discussed, which in more concrete terms include determining the behaviors that bring good results, observing/measuring those behaviors/results, providing clear and constructive feedback, and giving consistent reward and recognition for effort, improvement, and accomplishment. He was the kind of person we would all like to have in our organization. But, he had one problem in his use of this approach. Even though he was bright and made significant contributions to the organization on a daily basis, he was your basic "one-man band" in that he had no one reporting to him. He *was* the Engineering Department. The only thing that he found he could do was track his positive/negative statement ratio and while he could see an improvement in the way people responded to him, he wanted to do more.

One night at home, he received a call from a man asking him to coach a Little League Baseball team. His response was, "Are you sure that you don't have the wrong number? I've never played the game in any organized way and I'm sure that I would not be good at this because it requires coaching skills that I don't have."

The man answered, "Don't worry about that. These kids are the leftovers. All the good players have already been selected for other teams and this group is made up of those who want to wear a baseball uniform and be included in the activity. There's no pressure to win. In fact, we have a mercy rule in this league. If any team is behind by more than ten runs by the fifth inning, the game's over. We expect that this team will rarely make it beyond that. You're pretty much our last hope for a coach."

While he didn't actually jump at the opportunity, he accepted the challenge of trying to make the game of baseball fun for his little group of losers.

I was in his plant the following week and when I ran into him he said, "We need to talk." We met later in the day and he went over his plan. It was absolutely beautiful.

His team had only one practice and the assessment of their skills was awful. How could such a small group do one thing in so many wrong ways? Not one kid showed anything approaching proficiency in hitting the ball with a bat. He decided to make a list of the positives.

1) Just being there excited the kids. They loved wearing the uniforms and playing in games.

2) Since they rarely did anything pertaining to the game of baseball the same way twice, they have no bad habits to break.

3) They were very responsive to praise.

4) They were practically asking, what do you want me to do?

Item #4 gave the new coach a bit of a problem. He didn't know what he wanted them to do. He knew that they were never going to hit a ball unless they changed their method, but to what? He went to the library that night and checked out Ted Williams' book on hitting the ball. Who better to emulate?

After reading the entire book, he decided that they would start small. They would start with only two basic behaviors and build on that, when and if the kids became ready to move farther. The first was stance. The batter would face home plate, spread his feet to the approximate width of his shoulders, and hold the bat back in the ready position. The second behavior was to watch the ball until the bat connected with it. They took almost an entire session practicing this and helping the kids to get it right with the ball resting on a tee before facing an actual moving baseball.

The next session they had batting practice. An assistant coach sat beside the batting cage and started each kid off by reviewing his stance and swing. When he had it right, each player got ten swings at actual pitched balls.

NOTE: Here comes the answer to "How am I doing?"

The coach gave each batter feedback after every pitch and kept count of how many things each player did correctly by recording them on a separate piece of paper. After a boy had completed his ten swings, the coach gave him a brief recap of how he had done and after several batting sessions compared his totals with previous experiences. After accumulating a total of thirty behaviors done correctly, the player was in for special recognition. The coach would take the player's cap to his neighbor who owned an embroidery machine. The neighbor then embroidered a small baseball on the backside of the cap which the coach returned very ceremoniously to the player at the next practice. The kids loved it.

Another thing that our coach wanted to see was a player demonstrating approval for the performance of his peers. Bonus points were awarded for this and they began to get noisier with every practice.

For our purposes here, I relate only the things that the team did to improve hitting. The team addressed fielding, base running, and so on in much the same way. The results were remarkable and I would like to list a few of their accomplishments.

No Little Leaguer had ever hit a ball over the fence in this particular park. This team had thirty home runs and extra base hits that reached the fence were so common that no one bothered to count them. After the first five games, the mercy rule came into play quite often. However, this little team of losers was *giving* the mercy, not receiving it. They won the League Championship!

By that time, these players were making comments such as "We're the best Little League team on the planet!" and "We're going to go to the Little League World Series and kick Taiwan's butt." Well, they didn't go to the World

Series. They didn't win the State Championship either. The rules for the state competition called for one team from each league comprised of two players from every team in the league. Who knows how far this team could have gone if they could have remained a unit? They were disappointed, of course, but kids are resilient. The most important thing was the fact that they had a great experience and a lot of fun. They will remember that season for the rest of their lives and the adults associated with the team are richer for the experience.

Can work be as much fun? Of course it can. It not only *can* be fun, it *should* be fun. If you're my leader, make it fun. That's your job. My job is to be productive. If being productive is fun, I'll be more and more productive.

Do you think it's easier to make baseball fun than to make my job fun? Think about this. What is fun about baseball? Let's face it. Except for pitchers and catchers, baseball is mostly just standing around. An outfielder, for example, may go an entire game without having a ball hit to him. At bat, he could go zero for three by grounding out on the first pitch every time. That would put his actual playing time at around four or five minutes per game. Yet, some people play baseball at every opportunity. Why is he standing out in the hot sun when he could be home watching reruns? Why is playing baseball more fun than making vinegar or changing a fuel pump? The reason is that the conditions that exist around the activity have a great deal to do with how pleasant the experience is to be. There is absolutely no reason that we can't make work a fun activity. I've seen it happen.

One of the best examples of how things *should* work took place in a very large insurance company. For our purposes, I will focus on one department and how they made work enjoyable. They actually took the work out of work. The tasks required of that department really looked like drudgery to me. They processed insurance claims. They talked to customers on the phone and keyed information into computers. Their goal was to provide fast service and to satisfy customers. There were five or six departments doing the exact same job. Each department had two hundred to three hundred employees. As always, the first question was, What do you want me to do?

That question is not as easily answered as one might think. We had a meeting of all department managers and supervisors from these departments with an objective of determining the specific things that we wanted these people to do. My initial thought was that this shouldn't take long. How many different ways can a person answer the phone and key in data? As it turned out, there are many ways. One manager insisted that she could hear people smile when listening to them talk on the phone. Therefore, she required her employees to smile when talking on the phone. It was a long day, but we finally came up with a list of behaviors that everyone accepted as being critical to the job. We had answered the first question; now for the second: How am I doing?

Now let's narrow our focus a bit and look primarily at the things that happened in one particular department. They were all successful, but their methods varied so much that someone would have to write another book to describe all of the things that went on in all of the departments. One important precondition in this particular department was that the manager, Mary, was well ahead of most other people in how she related to her employees. Mary's employees liked to see her coming their way and her approval was important to them. She had a little bit of refining to do in terms of her desired ratio of four-to-one approving remarks to disapproving remarks, but her prep work was not as much as some of the others. She was ready to address the question of how am I doing?

Once the customer service employees understood the specific things that they needed to do, they wanted to

know when they were doing it correctly and when they weren't. This is where a great deal of creativity comes into play. I'm not that creative myself, but I certainly admire it in others and Mary had it.

These were the meetingest people that I have ever been around, which meant that the actual time available to walk around on the floor observing performance and giving feedback was greatly limited. Most of the manager's time was spent going to, sitting in, or returning from meetings. This lady decided that she could increase her contact with employees by varying her route in going to and returning from. She carried little cards with her at all times. Printed on the front of the card were the words, "Thanks for doing that just right." Then there was space to write in the action that the employee was doing correctly. They valued the cards and it was not unusual to see an employee decorate the walls of his or her cubicle with them.

The volume of calls handled was recorded electronically, so each customer service rep had reasonably current data on whether he/she was going too fast or too slow. Five calls per week were monitored for quality. That amounted to only about a 1 percent sample, but it provided meaningful information nonetheless.

Now for a little more creativity: Someone had gone to a local bookstore and noticed that they were about to throw out a life-sized cutout of Tim Allen, a rising star at the time of the television sitcom *Home Improvement*. Mr. Allen had apparently written a book and the cutout was among the promotional materials that were sent by the publisher. His image was rescued and brought to the customer service department where he served in a very useful capacity as a long-standing (in line, that is) customer. His function was to stand in line. Actually, he stood at the end of the line, and he did so all day, every day. The data on how many calls were currently on hold waiting for a customer service rep was available at all times. We considered these customers to be in line waiting their turn to be served. The waiting line should be kept at a minimum. Mr. Allen was moved backward or forward several times each day to indicate the current backlog of calls according to whether the backlog was larger (backward) or smaller (forward).

Now Mary was ready to address the question of what's in it for me? If you're as creative as Mary, there could be hundreds of answers to that question. There was one that I liked in particular. It was the victory lap. Whenever they exceeded a goal or surpassed some previous milestone, the reps would make a sign that stated their accomplishment. The group would hold the sign in the air while they circled the other departments in a shuffling kind of step. Personnel in the other departments would read the sign and applaud as they passed through. They weren't asked to do this; they just did it, because it was fun. They did it only two or three times before they went on to something new that was just as much fun. What these little breaks in the routine amounted to were short celebrations. It was something that took very little time and the group went back to the job with renewed enthusiasm. They were having fun at work!

 **LEADER'S LAST LAW: Let people take the time to celebrate their successes (even, if not especially, the little ones) if you want more and larger successes down the road.**

Epilogue

Thank you for reading this far. Most writers, I think, would like to end their work with a line that will move the reader to the point that he or she will never forget it. Unfortunately, *"Just Do It"* and *"Try it, you'll like it"* are already taken. So are *"Frankly My Dear, I don't give a damn," "I coulda been a contendah," "Play it again, Sam," "Nothing's too good for the man who shot Liberty Valance,"* and *"I'll make him an offer he can't refuse."* I guess I'm just going to have to go with *"You can't apologize to a dawg."* Good luck!

About ADI

ADI Aubrey Daniels International (ADI) helps the world's leading businesses use the scientifically proven laws of human behavior to promote workplace practices vital to long-term success. By developing strategies that reinforce critical work behaviors, ADI enables clients such as DaimlerChrysler Financial Services, Dollar General, and Blue Cross and Blue Shield, achieve and sustain consistently high levels of performance, building *profitable* habits™ within their organizations. ADI is led by Dr. Aubrey C. Daniels, the world's foremost authority on behavioral science in the workplace. Headquartered in Atlanta, the firm was founded in 1978.

Other ADI Titles

Measure of a Leader
Aubrey C. Daniels
James E. Daniels

A Good Day's Work
Alice Darnell Lattal
Ralph W. Clark

Other People's Habits
Aubrey C. Daniels

Bringing Out the Best in People
Aubrey C. Daniels

Performance Management: Changing Behavior That Drives Organizational Effectiveness (4th edition)
Aubrey C. Daniels
James E. Daniels

Precision Selling
Joseph S. Laipple

For more information call **1.800.223.6191**
or visit our Web site **www.aubreydaniels.com**

Register Your Book

Register your book and receive exclusive reader benefits. Visit the Web site below and click on the "Register Your Book" link at the top of the page. Registration is free.

www.pmanagementpubs.com

Tucker Wants to Hear from You

Send him an email at:
tucker.childers@comcast.net

Visit his Web site:
www.TuckerChilders.com